A Grammar of the Multitude

Copyright © 2004 Semiotext(e)
All rights reserved.

The italian edition was published from Rubbettino for Dottorato in Scienza Tecnologia e Società, Dipartimento di Sociologia e di Scienza Politica, Università della Calabria, Italy.

Special thanks for Giancarlo Ambrosino, Isabella Bertoletti, James Cascaito and Andrea Casson for copy editing.

Semiotext(e)
2571 W. Fifth Street
Los Angeles, CA 90057
www.semiotexte.org

Semiotext(e)
501 Philosophy Hall
Columbia University
New York, NY 10027

Design: Hedi El Kholti
The Index was established by Aventurina King.

ISBN-13: 978-1-58435-021-7
ISBN-10: 1-58435-021-0
Distributed by The MIT Press, Cambridge, Mass. and London, England
Printed in the United States of America

10 9 8 7 6 5 4 3

A Grammar of the Multitude

For an Analysis of Contemporary Forms of Life

Paolo Virno

Foreword by Sylvère Lotringer

Translated from the Italian
Isabella Bertoletti
James Cascaito
Andrea Casson

SEMIOTEXT(E) FOREIGN AGENTS SERIES

Contents

FOREWORD:

We, the Multitude

Paolo Virno's *A Grammar of the Multitude* is a short book, but it casts a very long shadow. Behind it looms the entire history of the labor movement and its heretical wing, Italian "workerism" (*operaismo*), which rethought Marxism in light of the struggles of the 1960s and 1970s. For the most part, though, it looks forward. Abstract intelligence and immaterial signs have become the major productive force in the "post-Fordist" economy we are living in and they are deeply affecting contemporary structures and mentalities. Virno's essay examines the increased mobility and versatility of the new labor force whose work-time now virtually extends to their entire life. The "multitude" is the kind of *subjective* configuration that this radical change is liberating, raising the political question of *what we are capable of.*

Operaismo (workerism) has a paradoxical relation to traditional Marxism and to the official labor movement because it refuses to consider work as the defining factor of human life. Marxist analysis assumes that what makes work alienating is capitalist exploitation, but operaists realized that it is rather *the reduction of life to work*. Paradoxically, "workerists" are *against* work, against the socialist ethics that used to exalt its dignity. They don't want to re-appropriate work ("take over the means of production") but reduce it. Trade unions or parties are concerned about wages and working conditions. They don't fight to change the workers' lot, at best they make it more tolerable. Workerists pressed for the reduction of labor time and the transformation of production through the application of technical knowledge and socialized intelligence.

In the mid-30s the leftist philosopher Simone Weil experienced the appalling abjection of the assembly line first hand by enlisting in a factory. She wondered whether Lenin or Stalin could ever have set foot in a workplace and celebrated workers' labor. "The problem is, therefore, quite clear," she concluded in *Oppression and Liberty* after renouncing Marxism and breaking up with the organized workers' movement. "It is a question of knowing whether it is possible to conceive of an organization of production" that wouldn't be "grinding down souls and bodies under oppression."[1] It was too early to achieve this goal through automation and her efforts remained isolated. It finally took the Italian Operaists in the late 50s to pick up where she left off.

Ideologically, Operaism was *made possible* by the Russian invasion of Hungary in 1956, which revealed the true nature of bureaucratic socialism. To young Italian intellectuals on the left of the left (among them Toni Negri and Mario Tronti) it became clear that the Soviet Union wasn't the Workers' Country, but a totalitarian form of capitalism. Around that time the first large emigration of Italian workers from the impoverished South to the industrial North proved even more unsettling. Instead of submitting to the new system of mass production, young unskilled workers ("mass-workers") bypassed established trade-unions, which privileged skilled workers, and furiously resisted the Ford assembly line. The Operaist movement took off in 1961 after the first massive labor confrontation in Turin. *Quaderni Rossi* ("Red Notebooks"), its first publication, analyzed the impact the young mass workers had on the labor force and the new "class composition" that emerged from recent capitalist transformations. *Classe Operaia* ("Working Class"), published in 1964, formulated a new political strategy, the refusal of work, challenging capital to develop its productive forces with new technology. This "strategy of refusal" (a seminal essay by Mario Tronti) was applied "inside" capitalist development, but "against it." It anticipated the post-68 analysis of capital by Félix Guattari and Gilles Deleuze in *Anti-Oedipus*, 1972, and brought Italian social thinkers and post-Structuralist French philosophers together in the mid-70s. What mass-workers objected to most was the transfer of human knowledge to the machines, reducing life to "dead labor." There was an existential dimension there, but active and creative. Their effort to change labor conditions was unknown to classical Marxism, mostly preoccupied with mechanisms of oppression and their effect on the working class.

In *Daybreak*, Nietzsche summoned European workers to "declare that henceforth *as a class* they are a human impossibility and not just, as is customary, a harsh and purposeless establishment." And he exhorted that "impossible class" to swarm out from the European beehive, "and with this act of emigration in the grand manner protest against the machine, against capital, and against the choice with which they are now threatened, of becoming *of necessity* either slaves of the state or slaves of a revolutionary party…" This celebration of exile can be found in Michael Hardt and Toni Negri's *Empire*, a best-seller among American Marxist academics and art critics ("A specter haunts the world and it is the specter of migration…") as well as in Virno's *A Grammar of the Multitude*, which it complements in its own way. This call retroactively found its model in the unorthodox and mobile migrant labor force of the Wobblies (International Workers of the World) who organized immigrant workers throughout the United States in the 1920s. (Hence the paradoxical fondness of operaists for the American workers' movement and America in general). Migration as a form of resistance also recalls Marx's essay on modern colonization, laborers in Europe deserting famines or factory work for free lands in the American West.[2] It took the inventiveness of Italian social thinkers to turn this cursory account of the workers' desire "to become independent landowners" into an anticipation of the postmodern multitude. While Hardt and Negri consider this kind of Exodus "a powerful form of class struggle," Virno cautions that desertion was "a transitory phase," an extended metaphor for the mobility of post-Fordist workers (European laborers worked in East Coast factories for a decade or two before moving on). A nuance, maybe, but significant. Unlike Hardt and Negri, Virno refrains from turning exile, or the multitude for that matter, let alone communism, into another splendid myth.

Autonomist theory is found in many places, including the United States, but the movement developed most powerfully in Italy where the 60s' movement extended well into the 70s. Breaking away from the orthodox and populist Marxism of Antonio Gramsci, founder of the Italian Communist Party, young Operaist intellectuals learned from the workers themselves what the reality of production was. They helped them create their organizations and confront the system of production head on through strikes and sabotage. This pragmatic and militant aspect of workerism sets Italian social thinkers apart. They opposed the hegemony of the Italian C.P. and Gramsci's strategy of small steps (the "war of position" within civil society) which led to Eurocommunism and the "historic compromise" with the governing Christian-Democrats (conservatives). Operaists were the first to question the centrality of the proletariat, cornerstone of the entire socialist tradition, and call for a reevaluation of the categories of class analysis. The notion of "changing class composition" introduced by Sergio Bologna allowed them to re-center the revolutionary struggle on the "new social subject" just emerging at the time both from the factory and the university.[3] The "Troubled Autumn" of 1969 was marked by the powerful offensive of mass-workers to obtain equality in salaries. Various workerist groups joined together to create a new organization, both a group and a magazine: *Potere Operaio* [Workers' Power]. It gathered a number of theorists like Mario Tronti, Toni Negri, Franco Piperno, Oreste Scalzone and Bologna. Their reformulation of Marxism became seminal for the entire autonomist movement. In 1974, the clandestine line of the Red Brigades clashed with the open forms of collective organization within Potere Operaio and led to the group's self-dissolution.

The workers' formidable pressure to control the cycle of production met with serious provocations from the secret services and the Christian-Democratic government, starting with the bombing of Piazza Fontana in Milan in 1969. Hastily attributed to the anarchists by the government, it justified an intense police repression of workers' organizations. This "strategy of tension" tore Italy apart and sent shock waves well into the 70s, verging on civil war. It triggered among factory workers in the Fiat factories the creation of underground terrorist groups—the "Red Brigades" and "Prima Linea" are the most well-known—targeting leaders of the industry and prominent political figures. The kidnapping of DC President Aldo Moro and his cold-blooded execution by the Red Brigades after the government broke off the negotiations, further upset the political balance in Italy.

In 1975 Potere Operaio was replaced by Autonomia, a large movement involving students, women, young workers and the unemployed. Their rhizomatic organization embodied every form of political behavior—anti-hierarchical, anti-dialectical, anti-representative—anticipated by Operaist thinkers. Autonomia wasn't any kind of normal political organization. Libertarian, neo-anarchistic, ideologically open and loosely organized by regions, it was respectful of political differences. Autonomist groups only cooperated in common public actions. Experimental and imaginative, the mass movement was a far cry from the tight terrorist groups taking "armed struggle" into their hands. In 1977, an autonomist student was murdered by the fascists in Rome and Autonomia exploded into the "Movement of 1977."[4] It swept the entire country, taking over the universities in Rome, Palermo and Naples, then in Florence, Turin and finally Bologna. It seemed as if they were about to take over Italy. What they would have done with it, Piperno recognized recently, they didn't really know. It was an inauspicious time for the movement to come of age. Challenged from its far left, the Communist Party used Moro's murder to eliminate Autonomia. Accused of being a shadow command for the "armed wing of the proletariat," all the autonomist leaders, including Negri, were arrested and jailed in April 1979. Others, like Piperno and Scalzone, went into exile (not by their own choice). Paolo Virno was on the editorial board of the influential autonomist magazine *Metropoli* and spent two years in jail before being cleared of all charges. (Twenty-five years later many autonomists are still in prison). He is now Dean in the Ethics of Communication at the University of Calabria where he gave the three seminars that make up this book in 2001.

Michael Hardt and Toni Negri's *Empire* makes no explicit reference to this period of social and political creativity, and there is a good reason for that. The American Left at the time was siding with Eurocommunism and considered Autonomia with suspicion. And yet the theses Negri defended then were hardly different from those he is developing today. So what has changed? (Paradoxically, the ghostly presence of Autonomia is felt far more strongly in *Empire* than in *A Grammar of the Multitude* where Paolo Virno confronts it head on.) The strategy proved enormously successful. The bulk of reviews and critical studies of *Empire* now far outweigh its own mass (some 500 pages). Unfortunately, few people will realize that the multitude isn't just a philosophical concept lifted from Spinoza—the democracy of the multitude—that it has a history under another name, and has been the object of vibrant collective experiments. They will never suspect either that the issues raised at the time are being picked up again, and that some kind of intellectual renaissance is presently occurring in Italy. What has been resurfacing recently in the United States with *Empire* isn't just another American cultural fad ("Empire" replacing "Globalization") but a bold and controversial social laboratory for the present. Virno's *A Grammar of the Multitude* is another sign of this return.

In "The Strategy of Refusal," published in 1965, Mario Tronti warned against focusing too much on the power of capital, or assume that it curbs labor power to its own ends. Workers are a class for themselves *before* being a class against capital. Actually, it is always capital that "seeks to use the worker's antagonistic will-to-struggle as a motor for its own development."[5] *Empire* develops the same argument: capitalism can only be *reactive* since it is the proletariat that "actually invents the social and productive forms that capital will be forced to adopt in the future."[6] It was the Italian workers' stubborn resistance to the Fordist rationalization of work, and not mere technological innovation, that forced capital to make a leap into the post-Fordist era of immaterial work.

Hardt and Negri strongly oppose any "hybrid thesis" that simultaneously emphasizes the creativity of capital and of the working class. In this respect they differ significantly from Deleuze and Guattari's analysis of capital, whose theory of flows they adopted (*Empire* clearly echoes *A Thousand Plateaus*). Deleuze and Guattari saw capital as fluid, inventive and adaptive, using every obstacle put in its path to rebound and move forward again. Yet they emphasized that it always fakes out in the end, never quite dares following through on its own movement. Because the limit of capitalism, like the stock-exchange, would be unregulated madness. Beating capital at its own game involves decoding its flows even further, or constantly displacing oneself in relation to them. They would certainly acknowledge as well that Italian capitalism was forced into a paradigm shift from the pressure of deterritorialized workers, but point out that it used this shift to regain the initiative and recode the working class into a less volatile social composition.

This is the conclusion Virno arrived at as well in *A Grammar of the Multitude*. Revisiting the tumultuous years of Autonomia, Virno realized that their struggle hadn't achieved their goals. The political confrontation only had a "semblance" of radical conflict, he says, because what autonomists were claiming wasn't really subversive in itself, just an anticipation of the post-Fordist mutation. Autonomists simply "had the misfortune of being treated [by those who still identified with the declining Fordist paradigm] as if it were a movement of marginal people and parasites," which it was not. And yet, Virno now estimates that it was just an "angry and coarse" version of the post-Fordist multitude because it often confused non-socialist demands (refusal of work, abolition of the state) with a proletarian revolution. ("A lot of people," he wryly notes, "were blathering on about revolution.") Autonomia was a *defeated* revolution, to which the post-Fordist paradigm was the answer.

But what kind of an "answer" is it? And in what way does the post-Ford era achieve what Autonomia failed to do by more direct means? The new proletariat didn't replace the working class, but extended it to all those whose labor is being exploited by capital. In the post-Fordist economy, surplus value is no longer extracted from labor materialized in a product, it resides in the discrepancy between paid and unpaid work—the idle time of the mind that keeps enriching, unacknowledged, the fruits of immaterial labor. As Marx wrote in *Grundrisse*, labor activity moves "*to the side* of the production instead of being its chief actor." The multitude is a force defined less by what it actually produces than by its virtuality, its *potential* to produce *and* produce itself. So is it really a gain over what existed before? Workers used to work in servile conditions, leaving them just enough time to replenish. Now their entire life is live labor, an invisible and indivisible commodity. Today all the multitude does is monitor signs on a screen. But machines are not "dead labor" anymore, they are part of the workers' "life labor" which now plugs into the "general intellect" dissiminating knowledge across the entire public sphere. The more creative and adaptable the workers are—the more *self-valorizing*—the more surplus of knowledge they can bring to the community at large. The multitude is a by-product of the technological mutation of the productive process just as the consumer class was a by-product of the metamorphosis of commodities from objects (*les choses*) to signs. In the post-Ford era, human communication has become the basis of productive cooperation in general. In purely social terms then, Virno is right. This is what autonomists were trying to achieve when they advocated "non-guaranteed" labor and nomadic ways in order to evade labor slavery and experience life to the fullest.

But is it also true in political terms? The multitude is a new category in political thought. But how "political" is it compared to the autonomia movement? It is, Virno suggests, open to plural experiences and searching for non-representative political forms, but "calmly and realistically," not from a marginal position. In a sense the multitude would finally fulfill Autonomia's motto—"The margins at the center"—through its active participation in socialized knowledge. Politics itself has changed anyway. Labor, politics and intellect are no longer separate, actually they have become interchangeable, and this is what gives the multitude a semblance of de-politization. Everything has become "performative." Virno brilliantly develops here his major thesis, an analogy between virtuosity (art, work, speech) and politics. They all are political because they all need an audience, a publicly organized space, which Marx calls "social cooperation," and a common language in which to communicate. And they all are a performance because they find in themselves, and not in any end product, their own fulfillment

Granted, this is not the assault on the Winter Palace, but autonomists never had that kind of performance in mind either. The contemporary multitude not being a class, it can't build a class consciousness of its own, let alone engage capital in a class struggle. And yet its very existence as multitude, distinct from "We, the People" (always predicated on the State) speaks of "the crisis of the form-of-state" itself. *A Grammar of the Multitude* dwells at length on the changing nature of contemporary forms of life, but it doesn't elaborate further on this crisis of the nation-state, simply attributes it to the "centrifugal character of the multitude." It is at this point that *Empire* comes in.

Hardt and Negri embrace as well the notion of a "postmodern" social class, but they try and offset its increasing political disaffection by drastically changing its scale and ideological horizon. For them it isn't just the crisis of the form-of-state that the multitude announces, but of the very form-of-empire presently being shaped by globalization. *Empire* is a powerful political synthesis of the momentous transformations that are relegating parties and nation-states to a subsidiary role. Advanced capitalism is de-regulating markets, forcing modern states to transfer their sovereignty to a superior entity, an "acephalous supranational order" made of a pyramid of transnational corporations, trans-political organizations and advanced capitalist nations led by the only remaining superpower, the United States. (The United States may well be imperialistic, but it is *not* Empire). Sovereign states losing their power of mediation, a new constitutional process is beginning to emerge, allowing for enforceable international regulations to proliferate and more complex forms of hierarchy and inequality to replace the traditional antagonism between state and society, ruling class and proletariat. As a result the kind of multitude Hardt and Negri have in mind is of a fairly different order than Virno's. Empire isn't an "epochal shift" brought about by post-Fordist economy and the imposition of a transnational universal order, it is another concession extracted by the entire multitude fronting for the old working class. Empire, still rising, already harbors the seeds of its own destruction.

It is a bold claim that aims to shake Empire at its very foundation. Placing Virno's multitude at the heart of Empire opens up an entirely new political paradigm, while conveniently keeping class struggle as the motor of history. The dwindling of the nation-states, though, could well have weakened the revolutionary movement, and many would argue that it did, but Hardt and Negri are emphatic that the "new social class" was indeed bolstered by the emergence of supranational structures. So they wouldn't oppose globalization, actually welcome Empire as Autonomia praised America. Clearly, they needed an oversize enemy to build up the defeated Italian movement into a *global counter-power*.

The global multitude is hybrid, fluid, mutant, deterritorialized, just like immaterial workers of the postmodern world, and yet, in mysterious ways, it is supposed to encompass the world poor which replaced the working-class at the bottom of the ladder. (Traditionally the workers' movement has been distrustful of the unorganized lumpenproletariat). The poor are not immaterial, they all-too-material themselves in their wretchedness, and Negri often evokes in general terms their *kairos* of "poverty and love." (The rise of Christianity during the decline of the Roman Empire runs throughout much of *Empire* as an infectious, but problematic, analogy to revolutionary desire). For Hardt and Negri, the multitude is this new social class that removes itself from nations and parties to meet head on the challenge of Empire. "In its will to be-against and its desire for liberation," the multitude "must push through Empire to come out the other side."[7]

The other side, of course, is so much better. Paradise is another example. The problem is that a multitude capable of doing such a feat doesn't exist—or doesn't exist yet. At best, it remains a taunting hypothesis, and a promising field of investigation for whoever wants to follow the lead.[8] But the idea that capital could simply be "destroyed" by such an essentialist notion is a bit hard to swallow. Unlike the industrial proletariat, the postmodern multitude doesn't make up "a workers' army," the kind that is readily launched against capital, or against Empire. (The worker's army didn't exactly move against the State during May 1968 in France). The "other side" belongs, poetically, to the panoply of endangered ideologies. That an alternative to the contemporary imperial order is "necessary"—the multitude *must* push through like a battering ram—doesn't make its existence any more tangible. But Hardt and Negri are already busily thinking "how concrete instances of class struggle can actually arise, and moreover form a coherent program of struggle, a constituent power adequate to the destruction of the enemy and the construction of a new society. The question is really how the body of the multitude can configure itself as a telos."[9]

The telos, in other words, *precedes* the multitude, and for the most part replaces it. No wonder *Empire* was so well received in America, and among the people who, incidentally, some twenty-five years ago, looked the other way as the Italian movement was being brutally crushed. (The embattled *Italy: Autonomia* issue of *Semiotext(e)*, now reissued, was first published in 1980, barely one year after the autonomists' arrests.) Frederic Jameson hailed *Empire* as "the first great theoretical synthesis of the new millennium" and Etienne Balibar, praising Negri's "hyper-Marxism," acknowledged that it laid the foundations for "a new teleology of class struggles and militancy." As for Slavoj Zizek, his conviction was that "if this book were not written, it would have to be invented." Zizek may even be right there. Didn't Nietzsche say that thinking is always *untimely*?

What is exciting, actually, in *Empire*, is the question it implicitly raises by globalizing the multitude, not the assumption that it is "the productive force that sustains Empire and calls for and makes necessary its destruction." This war is purely mythical, and so is the destruction of capital. That's why their confrontation quickly takes on an allegorical dimension, a war between *two principles*. The multitude being as immaterial as the work it produces, it is dressed, Hardt and Negri write, "in simplicity, and also innocence." It is prophetic and productive, an "absolutely positive force" capable of being changed "into an absolute democratic power." Even its will to destruction would eventually become "love and community." Evil Empire, on the other hand, the con-enemy, is just an "empty shell," a giant with clay-feet, vicious, abusive, controlling, a predator always engaged in "an operation of absolute violence" (principles are necessarily *absolute*). Imperial command is nothing but an "abstract and empty unification," a "parasitical machine" that only lives off the vitality of the multitude and constitutes "the negative residue, the fallback" of its operation. "A parasite that saps the strength of its host, however, can endanger its own existence. The functioning of imperial power," Hardt and Negri conclude, "is ineluctably linked to its decline."[10] Why call for a counter-power then?

Because History can't wait. There is a question that keeps coming up again and again throughout Negri's writings, and it is the irreducibility of the moment of decision. Although he pays lip service to the tradition of "vitalist materialism"—Nietzsche, Bergson, Deleuze—the "will to power" or the "élan vital" obviously aren't enough for a lusty Leninist. These always run the risk, he writes, of "getting caught in the sophisms of the bad infinite: an infinite that dilutes the intensity of the decision…"[11] Without a telos, a big narrative, a decision would mean nothing anyway. *Empire* involves an original kind of class struggle: *a struggle looking for a class.* For Virno it would be just the reverse: a class looking for a struggle. But Hardt and Negri already know what kind of class they are looking for. Their real purpose is to jump-start the revolutionary machine. They quote Spinoza: "The prophet produces its own people." They want to produce their own multitude, but they are not exactly sure it will work. They even admit it candidly: "It is not at all clear that this prophetic function can effectively address our political needs and sustain a manifesto of the postmodern revolution against Empire..."[12] A *postmodern* revolution, no less. The class struggle was postmodern too.

Virno doesn't have any telos up his sleeve, no ready-made program for the multitude—certainly not coming out "the other side." It's been tried before, didn't turn out so well. Why should a "postmodern revolution" be any different? Anyone who cares for the multitude should first figure out what it is about and what could be expected from it, not derive its mode of being from some revolutionary essence. The ultimate goal of Virno's inventive inventory is "rescuing political action from its current paralysis."*Empire* is trying that too, but a straw fight won't do—The Multitude Strikes Back…

Virno may be onto something when he suggests that Post-Fordism is "the communism of capital." It doesn't say that there is no more fights in sight, that post-Fordism brought us "communism." Fights should be expected, but not a war that would allegedly destroy the enemy. A *combat* rather, meant to strengthen some forces present in capital, and join them with other forces in order to form a new communist ensemble. This is what Virno has been attempting to provide: the description of a combat, a cartography of virtualities made possible by post-Fordism, elements in contemporary life that could eventually be mobilized. The problem is not to destroy capital or Empire—destroy, they say—but bolster one's own power. What is a body *capable of?*

"The communism of capital": there is as much communism in capital *as capital is capable of* too: abolition of work, dissolution of the state, etc. But communism in any shape or form would require equality, and this, capital is incapable of providing. Post-Fordism therefore can only satisfy the *demands* of a virtual communism. A communality of generalized intellect without material equality. How "communistic" can that be? And can this *virtual* communism be enough to turn subjected "people" into a freer "multitude"? This is what Empire is claiming to achieve, but the multitude isn't exactly thriving beyond the First World, or below. In under-developing countries the new labor class is finding freedom through uprooting and over-exploitation. Inequalities everywhere are growing exponentially, and so is cynicism, not especially of the creative kind.

This is no reason for disenchantment. One of the virtues of Autonomia is that it was never afraid of claiming out loud: "We are the front of luxury." At the time the exploited proletariat was still considered to be the repository of revolutionary wisdom. But only those who are free from slavery can dare imagine what being really free would be. This is what the Italians were trying to experiment with before Autonomia was "defeated," and that's what they are exploring again today through a lively intellectual debate. The idea of a multitude is part of this on-going project. It is a luxury that we should be able to afford: the luxury of imagining a future that would actively bring together everything we are capable of. These virtualities are present within capital in ambivalent and reversible features that are just waiting to be liberated. Immaterial workers are mobile and detached, adaptable, curious, opportunistic and cynical, also toward institutions; they are inventive and share knowledge through communication and language; they are mostly de-politicized, also disobedient. The multitude is an "amphibious" category that can veer toward "opposing developments," or come to nothing, so a combat is constantly raging—not with Empire, *within itself.* A combat that first "defines the composition of forces in the combatant,"[13] not its victory over an exterior enemy.

Capital affords us to project ahead, work it from within, knowing all too well that it will be quick to instrumentalize any creative move, turning it into binary oppositions, however radical thay claim to be, proven recipes that failed repeatedly *because they have become inadequate to think the complexity of the contemporary reality*. The paradoxical positions autonomists have assumed in relation to work, or the strategic embrace of Empire by Hard and Negri, are part of a luxury of thinking ahead, unimpeded, which has become such a precious commodity in a world squeezed between mediocrity and self-satisfied gloom. So no one could reproach them for thinking that, only for *not thinking enough*, falling back too soon on the quick revolutionary fix that will please everyone and just reinforce a cozy feeling of powerlessness.

Capital doesn't have to be "destroyed." It is self-destructive enough, but not the way Hardt and Negri imagined it. Because it never stops provoking resistance to its own rule."It is doubtful that the joys of capitalism are enough to liberate the people," Deleuze wrote in 1991.[14] "Those who keep invoking the bloody failure of socialism don't seem to consider as a failure the present state of the global capitalist market, with the bloody inequalities it involves, the populations pushed off the market, etc. It's been a long time since the American 'revolution' has failed, even before the Soviet's did. The situations and revolutionary attempts are generated by capitalism itself and they are not going to disappear." Capitalism itself is revolutionary because it keeps fomenting inequality and provoking unrest. It also keeps providing its own kind of "communism" both as a vaccine, preventing further escalation, and an incentive to go beyond its own limitations. The multitude responds to both and can go either way, absorbing the shocks or multiplying the fractures that will occur in unpredictable ways.

A specter haunts the world and it is the specter of capital...

—Sylvère Lotringer

---

1. Simone Weil, *Oppression and Liberty*. Amherst: The University of Massachussets Press, 1958, p. 56

2. In Karl Marx, *Capital* I, "The modern theory of colonization."

3. Cf. Sergio Bologna, "The Tribe of Moles," in *Italy: Autonomia. Post-Political Politics*. New York: *Semiotext(e)*, III, 3, 1980, pp. 36-61. Edited by Sylvère Lotringer and Christian Marazzi.

4. Cf. Bifo, "Anatomy of Autonomy," in *Italy: Autonomia*, op. cit., pp. 148-170.

5. See Mario Tronti, "The Strategy of refusal," in *Italy: Autonomia, op. cit.*, pp. 28-35.

6. Michael Hardt and Antonio Negri, *Empire*. Cambridge, Mass.: Harvard University Press, 2000, p. 268.

7. *Empire, op. cit.*, p. 218.

8. See Christian Marazzi, "Denaro e Guerra." [Money and War]. In Andrea Fumagalli, Christian Marazzi & Adelino Zanini, *La Moneta nell Impero*. Verona: Ombre Corte, 2003. The crash of the new economy signals the resistance of the multitude to the financialization of the general intellect. Also Breit Nelson, "The Market and the Police: Finance Capital in the Permanent Global War." (Unpublished.)

9. *Empire, op. cit.*, pp. 403-4.

10. *Empire, op. cit.*, pp. 413, 344, 361, 63, 361.

11. Antonio Negri, *Kairos, Alma Venus, Multitude*. Paris: Calmann Levy, 2000, p. 194.

12. *Empire, op.cit.*, p. 63.

13. On "war"and "combat," see Gilles Deleuze, *Critical and Clinical*. Minneapolis: University of Minnesota Press, 1997, p. 132.

14. Gilles Deleuze and Félix Guattari, "Nous avons inventé la ritournelle" [We have invented the refrain], *Le Nouvel Observateur*, September 1991. In Gilles Deleuze, *Two Regimes of Madness*. New York: Semiotext(e), 1974. (Forthcoming.)

INTRODUCTION

People vs. Multitude: Hobbes and Spinoza

I maintain that the concept of "multitude," as opposed to the more familiar concept of "people," is a crucial tool for every careful analysis of the contemporary public sphere. One must keep in mind that the choice between "people" and "multitude" was at the heart of the practical controversies (the establishing of centralized modern States, religious wars, etc.) and of the theoretical-philosophical controversies of the seventeenth century. These two competing concepts, forged in the fires of intense clashes, played a primary role in the definition of the political-social categories of the modern era. It was the notion of "people" which prevailed. "Multitude" is the losing term, the concept which got the worst of it. In describing the forms of associative life and of the public spirit of the newly constituted great States, one no longer spoke of multitude, but of people. But we need to ask whether, today, at the end of a long cycle, the old dispute has not been opened up once again; whether, today, now that the political theory of the modern era is going through a radical crisis, this once defeated notion is not displaying extraordinary vitality, thus taking its dramatic revenge.

The two polarities, people and multitude, have Hobbes and Spinoza as their putative fathers. For Spinoza, the *multitudo* indicates a *plurality which persists as such* in the public scene, in collective action, in the handling of communal affairs, without converging into a One, without evaporating within a centripetal form of motion. Multitude is the form of social and political existence for the many, seen as being many: a permanent form, not an episodic or interstitial form. For Spinoza, the *multitudo* is the architrave of civil liberties (Spinoza, *Tractatus Politicus*).

Hobbes *detests*—and I am using here, after due consideration, a passionate, not very scientific word—the multitude; he rages against it. In the social and political existence of the many, seen as being many, in the plurality which does not converge into a synthetic unity, he sees the greatest danger of a "supreme empire"; that is to say, for that *monopoly of political decision-making* which is the State. The best way to understand the significance of a concept—multitude, in this case—is to examine it with the eyes of one who has fought it tenaciously. The person who grasps all the implications and the nuances of a concept is precisely the one who wishes to expunge it from the theoretical and practical horizon.

Before giving a brief explanation of the way in which Hobbes portrays the detested multitude, it is good to determine exactly the goal being pursued here. I wish to show that the category of the multitude (precisely as it is treated by its sworn enemy, Hobbes) helps to explain a certain number of contemporary social behaviors. After the centuries of the "people" and then those of the State (nation-State, centralized State, etc.), the opposing polarity returns at last to manifest itself, having been annulled at the dawning of the modern era. Multitude seen as the last cry of social, political and philosophical theory? Perhaps. An entire gamut of considerable phenomena—linguistic games, forms of life, ethical inclinations, salient characteristics of production in today's world—will end up to be only slightly, or not at all, comprehensible, unless understood as originating from the mode of being of the *many*. To investigate this mode of being, one must have recourse to a rather varied kind of conceptual orchestration: anthropology, philosophy of language, criticism of political economics, ethics. One must circumnavigate the multitude-continent, changing frequently the angle of perspective.

This having been said, let us look briefly at the way in which Hobbes delineates, in his role as perspicacious adversary, the mode of being of the "many." For Hobbes, the decisive political clash is the one which takes place between multitude and people. The modern public sphere can have as its barycenter *either* one *or* the other. Civil war, always threatening, has its logical form in this alternative. The concept of people, according to Hobbes, is strictly correlated to the existence of the State; furthermore, it is a reverberation, a reflection of the State: if there is a State, then there are people. In the absence of the State, there are no people. In the *De Cive*, in which the horror of the multitude is exposed far and wide, we read: "The *People* is somewhat that is *one*, having *one will*, and to whom one action may be attributed" (Hobbes, *De Cive*, Chap. XII, section VIII).

The multitude, for Hobbes, is inherent in the "state of nature;" therefore, it is inherent in that which precedes the "body politic." But remote history can re-emerge, like a "repressed experience" which returns to validate itself, in the crises which sometimes shake state sovereignty. Before the State, there were the many; after the establishment of the State, there is the One-people, endowed with a single will. The multitude, according to Hobbes, shuns political unity, resists authority, does not enter into lasting agreements, never attains the *status* of juridical person because it never transfers its own natural rights to the sovereign. The multitude inhibits this "transfer" by its very mode of being (through its plural character) and by its mode of behaving. Hobbes, who was a great writer, emphasizes with admirable refinement, how the multitude is anti-state, but, precisely for this reason, anti-people: "the *People*, stirring up the *Citizens* against the *City*, that is to say, the *Multitude* against the *People*" (Hobbes, ibid.). The contrast between the two concepts is carried here to full range: if there are people, there is no multitude; if there is a multitude, there are no people. For Hobbes and for the seventeenth century apologists for state sovereignty, multitude is a purely negative borderline concept; that is to say, it is identified with the risks which weigh upon stateness; it is the debris which can sometimes jam the "big machine." It is a negative concept this multitude: it is that which did not make itself fit to become people, in as much as it virtually contradicts the state monopoly of political decision making; in brief, it is a regurgitation of the "state of nature" in civil society.

Exorcized plurality: the "private" and the "individual"

How has the multitude survived the creation of the centralized States? Through what concealed and feeble forms has it made itself known after the full affirmation of the modern concept of sovereignty? Where is its echo heard? Stylizing the question to the extreme, let us try to identify the ways in which the *many*, seen as being *many*, have been understood in liberal thought and in democratic-socialist thought (thus, in political traditions which have had their indisputable point of reference in the unity of the people).

In liberal thought, the uneasiness provoked by the "many" is toned down by means of having recourse to the pairing of the terms public-private. The multitude, which is the polar opposite of the people, takes on the slightly ghostly and mortifying features of the so-called *private*. Incidentally, even the public-private dyad itself, before becoming something indisputable, had been forged through tears and blood during a thousand theoretical and practical disputes; it is maintained, therefore, by a complex set of consequences. What could be more normal for us than to speak of public experience and of private experience? But this bifurcation was not always taken for granted. The lack of indisputability is interesting because, today, we are perhaps living in a new seventeenth century, or in an age in which the old categories are falling apart and we need to coin new ones. Many concepts which still seem extravagant and unusual to us—the notion of non-representative democracy, for example—are perhaps already tending to drum up a new kind of common sense, in order to aspire, in turn, to become "obvious." But let us return to the point. "Private" signifies not only something personal, not only something which concerns the inner life of this person or that; private signifies, above all, *deprived of*: deprived of a voice, deprived of a public presence. In liberal thought, the multitude survives as a private dimension. The many are aphasic and far removed from the sphere of common affairs.

In democratic-socialist thought, where is it that we find an echo of the archaic multitude? Perhaps in the pairing of the terms collective-individual. Or, better yet, in the second of these terms, in the individual dimension. The people are the collective; the multitude is concealed by the presumed impotence, as well as by the immoderate uneasiness, of single individuals. The individual is the irrelevant remainder of divisions and multiplications which are carried out somewhere far from the individual. In terms of what can be called individual in the strictest sense, the individual seems indescribable. Just as the multitude is indescribable within the democratic-socialist tradition.

At this point I should speak in advance of an opinion which will appear on several occasions in what I will have to say later. I believe that in today's forms of life one has a direct perception of the fact that the coupling of the terms public-private, as well as the coupling of the terms collective-individual, can no longer stand up on their own, that they are gasping for air, burning themselves out. This is just like what is happening in the world of contemporary production, provided that production—loaded as it is with *ethos*, culture, linguistic interaction—not give itself over to econometric analysis, but rather be understood as a broad-based experience of the world. That which was rigidly subdivided now blends together and is superimposed upon itself. It is difficult to say where collective experience ends and individual experience begins. It is difficult to separate public experience from so-called private experience. In this blurring of borders, even the two categories of *citizen* and of *producer* fail us; or they become only slightly dependable as categories, even though they were so important in Rousseau, Smith, Hegel, and even in Marx himself (though being nothing more than a polemical butt).

The contemporary multitude is composed neither of "citizens" nor of "producers;" it occupies a middle region between "individual and collective;" for the multitude, then, the distinction between "public" and "private" is in no way validated. And it is precisely because of the dissolution of the coupling of these terms, for so long held to be obvious, that one can no longer speak of a *people* converging into the unity of the state. While one does not wish to sing out-of-tune melodies in the post-modern style ("multiplicity is good, unity is the disaster to beware of"), it is necessary, however, to recognize that the multitude does not clash with the One; rather, it redefines it. Even the many need a form of unity, of being a One. But here is the point: this unity is no longer the State; rather, it is language, intellect, the communal faculties of the human race. The One is no longer a *promise*, it is a *premise*. Unity is no longer something (the State, the sovereign) towards which things converge, as in the case of the people; rather, it is taken for granted, as a background or a necessary precondition. The many must be thought of as the individualization of the universal, of the generic, of the shared experience. Thus, in a symmetric manner, we must conceive of a One which, far from being something conclusive, might be thought of as the base which authorizes differentiation or which allows for the political-social existence of the *many* seen as being *many*. I say this only in order to emphasize that present-day reflection on the category of multitude does not allow for rapturous simplifications or superficial abbreviations; instead, such reflection must confront some harsh problems: above all the logical problem (which needs to be reformulated, not removed) of the relationship of One/Many.

Three approaches to the Many

The concrete definitions of the contemporary multitude can be placed in focus through the development of three thematic units. The first of these is very Hobbesian: the dialectic between fear and the search for security. It is clear that even the concept of "people" (in its seventeenth century articulations, either liberal or democratic-socialist) is centered around certain strategies developed to foil danger and to obtain protection. I will maintain (in today's presentation) that on the empirical and conceptual levels, the forms of fear have failed, together with the corresponding types of refuge to which the notion of "people" has been connected. What prevails instead is a dialectic of dread-refuge which is quite different: one which defines several characteristic traits of today's multitude. Fear-security: this is the grid or litmus paper which is philosophically and sociologically relevant in order to show how the figure of the multitude is not all "peaches, cream and honey," in order to identify what specific poisons are lurking in this figure. The multitude is a *mode of being*, the prevalent mode of being today: but, like all modes of being, it is *ambivalent*, or, we might say, it contains within itself both loss and salvation, acquiescence and conflict, servility and freedom. The crucial point, however, is that these alternative possibilities have a peculiar physiognomy, different from the one with which they appeared within the people/general-will/State cluster.

The second theme, which I will deal with in the next seminar, is the relation between the concept of multitude and the crisis of the ancient tripartitioning of human experience into Labor, Politics, Thought. This has to do with a subdivision proposed by Aristotle, then taken up again in the twentieth century, above all by Hannah Arendt, and encysted until very recently within our notion of common sense. This is a subdivision which now, however, has fallen apart.

The third thematic unit consists of sifting through several categories in order to be able to say something about the *subjectivity of the multitude*. Above all, I will examine three of these categories: the principle of individuation, and the categories of idle talk and curiosity. The first of these categories is an austere and wrongly neglected metaphysical question: what is it that renders an individual identity individual? The other two categories, instead, have to do with daily life. It was Heidegger who conferred the dignity of philosophical concepts upon the categories of idle talk and curiosity. Even though my argument will avail itself of certain pages of *Being and Time*, the manner in which I will speak of these categories is substantially non-Heideggerian, or actually anti-Heideggerian.

Forms of Dread and Refuge

Day One

Beyond the coupling of the terms fear/anguish

The dialectic of dread and refuge lies at the center of the "Analytic of the Sublime," a section of the *Critique of Judgment* (Kant, Book II, Part I). According to Kant, when I observe a terrifying snowslide while I myself am in safety, I am filled with a pleasing sense of security mixed together, however, with the heightened perception of my own helplessness. *Sublime* is precisely the word for this twofold feeling which is partially contradictory. With my starting point being the empirical protection which I have benefited from by chance, I am made to ask myself what it is that could guarantee an absolute and systematic protection for my existence. That is to say, I ask myself what it is that might keep me safe, not from one given danger or another, but from the risk inherent in my very being in this world. Where is it that one can find unconditional refuge? Kant answers: in the moral "I," since it is precisely there that one finds something of the non-contingent, or of the realm above the mundane. The transcendent moral law protects my person in an *absolute* way, since it places the value which is due to it above finite existence and its numerous dangers. The feeling of the sublime (or at least one of its incarnations) consists of taking the relief I feel for having enjoyed a fortuitous place of refuge and transforming it into a search for the unconditional security which only the moral "I" can guarantee.

I have mentioned Kant for one specific reason: because he offers a very clear model of the world in which the dialectic of dread/refuge has been conceived in the last two centuries. There is a sharp bifurcation here: on one hand, a particular danger (the snowslide, the malevolent attentions of the Department of the Interior, the loss of one's job, etc.); on the other hand, there is the absolute danger connected to our very being in this world. Two forms of protection (and of security) correspond to these two forms of risk (and of dread). In the presence of a real disaster, there are concrete remedies (for example, the mountain refuge when the snowslide comes crashing down). Absolute danger, instead, requires protection from … the world itself. But let us note that the "world" of the human animal can not be put on the same level as the *environment* of the non-human animal, or rather, of the circumscribed *habitat* in which the latter animal finds its way around perfectly well on the basis of specialized instincts. There is always something *indefinite* about the world; it is laden with contingencies and surprises; it is a vital context which is never mastered once and for all; for this reason, it is a source of permanent insecurity. While relative dangers have a "first and last name," absolute dangerousness has no exact face and no unambiguous content.

The Kantian distinction between the two types of risk and security is drawn out in the distinction, traced by Heidegger, between *fear* and *anguish*. Fear refers to a very specific fact, to the familiar snowslide or to the loss of one's job; anguish, instead, has no clear cause which sparks it off. In the pages of Heidegger's *Being and Time* (Heidegger, § 40) anguish is provoked purely and simply by our being exposed to the world, by the uncertainty and indecision with which our relation to this world manifests itself. Fear is always circumscribed and nameable; anguish is ubiquitous, not connected to distinctive causes; it can survive in any given moment or situation. These two forms of dread (fear and anguish), and their corresponding antidotes, lend themselves to a historical-social analysis.

The distinction between circumscribed fear and unspecified fear is operative where there are substantial communities constituting a channel which is capable of directing our praxis and collective experience. It is a channel made of repetitive, and therefore comfortable, usages and customs, made of a consolidated *ethos*. *Fear* situates itself inside the community, inside its forms of life and communication. *Anguish*, on the other hand, makes its appearance when it distances itself from the community to which it belongs, from its shared habits, from its well-known "linguistic games," and then penetrates into the vast world. Outside of the community, fear is ubiquitous, unforeseeable, constant; in short, anguish-ridden. The counterpart of fear is that security which the community can, in principle, guarantee; the counterpart of anguish (or of its showing itself to the world as such) is the shelter procured from religious experience.

So, the dividing line between fear and anguish, between relative dread and absolute dread, is precisely what has failed. The concept of "people," even with its many historical variations, is closely bound to the clear separation between a habitual "inside" and an unknown and hostile "outside." The concept of "multitude," instead, hinges upon the ending of such a separation. The distinction between fear and anguish, just like the one between relative shelter and absolute shelter, is groundless for at least three reasons.

The first of these reasons is that one can not speak reasonably of substantial communities. In today's world, impulsive changes do not overturn traditional and repetitive forms of life; what they do is to come between individuals who by now have gotten used to no longer having fixed customs, who have gotten used to sudden change, who have been exposed to the unusual and to the unexpected. What we have, then, at every moment and no matter what, is a reality which is repeatedly innovated. It is therefore not possible to establish an actual distinction between a stable "inside" and an uncertain and telluric "outside." The permanent mutability of the forms of life, and the training needed for confronting the unchecked uncertainty of life, lead us to a direct and continuous relation with the world as such, with the imprecise context of our existence.

What we have, then, is a complete overlapping of fear and anguish. If I lose my job, of course I am forced to confront a well defined danger, one which gives rise to a specific kind of dread; but this real danger is immediately colored by an unidentifiable anguish. It is fused together with a more general disorientation in the presence of the world in which we live; it is identified with the absolute insecurity which lives in the human animal, in as much as the human animal is lacking in specialized instincts. One might say: fear is always anguish-ridden; circumscribed danger always makes us face the general risk of being in this world. If the substantial communities once hid or muffled our relationship with the world, then their dissolution now clarifies this relationship for us: the loss of one's job, or the change which alters the features of the functions of labor, or the loneliness of metropolitan life—all these aspects of our relationship with the world assume many of the traits which formerly belonged to the kind of terror one feels outside the walls of the community. We would need to find a new term here, different from "fear" or "anguish," a term which would take the fusion of these two terms into account. What comes to mind for me is the term *uncanny*. But it would take too much time here to justify the use of this term (Virno, *Mondanità*: 65-7).

Let us move on to the second critical approach. According to traditional explanations, fear is a *public* feeling, while anguish pertains to the individual who has been isolated by a fellow human being. In contrast to fear (which is provoked by a danger pertaining virtually to many members of the community and which can be resisted with the help of others), the anguished feeling of being lost evades the public sphere and is concerned only with the so-called interior nature of the individual. This type of explanation has become completely unreliable. For certain reasons, in fact, it must be overturned. Today, all forms of life have the experience of "not feeling at home," which, according to Heidegger, would be the origin of anguish. Thus, there is nothing more shared and more common, and in a certain sense more *public*, than the feeling of "not feeling at home." No one is less isolated than the person who feels the fearful pressure of the indefinite world. In other words, that feeling in which fear and anguish converge is immediately the *concern of many*. One could say, perhaps, that "not feeling at home" is in fact a distinctive trait of the concept of the multitude, while the separation between the "inside" and the "outside," between fear and anguish, is what earmarked the Hobbesian (and not only Hobbesian) idea of people. The people are one, because the substantial community collaborates in order to sedate the fears which spring from circumscribed dangers. The multitude, instead, is united by the risk which derives from "not feeling at home," from being exposed omnilaterally to the world.

Now let us consider the third and last critical observation, perhaps the most radical. It concerns the same dread/refuge coupling. What is mistaken in this coupling is the idea that we *first* experience a sense of dread and, only *then*, we set ourselves the task of procuring a source of refuge. These stimulus-response or cause-effect models are completely out of place. Rather, one should believe that the original experience would be that of procuring some means of refuge. Above all, we protect ourselves; then, when we are intent on protecting ourselves, we focus on identifying the dangers with which we may have to concern ourselves. Arnold Gehlen used to say that survival, for the human animal, was an oppressive task, and that in order to confront this task we need, above all, to mitigate the disorientation which results from the fact that we are not in possession of a fixed "environment" (Gehlen, *Man: His Nature*). Within one's living context, this groping attempt to cope with life is basic. Even as we seek to have a sense of orientation which will allow us to protect ourselves, we also perceive, often in retrospect, various forms of danger.

There is more to the story. Not only does danger define itself starting with the original search for refuge, but, and this is the truly crucial point, danger manifests itself for the most part *as* a specific form of refuge. If we look carefully, we see that danger consists of a horrifying strategy of salvation (one need only think of the cult of some ethnic "enclave"). The dialectic between danger and refuge is resolved, in the end, in the dialectic between alternative forms of protection. In contrast to the *sources of refuge to be feared* we find the *second rank sources of refuge*, those which are capable of serving as an antidote to the poisons of the former sources of refuge. From the historical and sociological point of view, it is not difficult to see that evil expresses itself precisely as a horrible response to the risk inherent in this world, as a dangerous search for protection: we need only think about the propensity for entrusting oneself to a sovereign (either in the flesh, or one of those operetta types, it doesn't matter), or about the feverish elbowing to get to the top in one's career, or about xenophobia. We could also say: being truly anguish-ridden is just a certain way of confronting anguish. Let me repeat: what is decisive here is the choice between different strategies of reassurance, the opposition between extremely different forms of refuge. For this reason, let me say in passing, it is foolish either to overlook the theme of security, or (and this is even more foolish) to brandish it without further qualification (not recognizing the true danger in this very theme, or in certain of its types).

The experience of the contemporary (or, if your prefer, of the post-Fordist) multitude is primarily rooted in this modification of the dialectic of dread-refuge. The *many*, in as much as they are *many*, are those who share the feeling of "not feeling at home" and who, in fact, place this experience at the center of their own social and political praxis. Furthermore, in the multitude's mode of being, one can observe with the naked eye a continuous *oscillation* between different, sometimes diametrically opposed, strategies of reassurance (an oscillation which the people, however, do not understand, since they are an integral part of the sovereign States).

Common places and "general intellect"

In order to have a better understanding of the contemporary notion of multitude, it will be useful to reflect more profoundly upon which essential resources might be the ones we can count on for protection from the dangerousness of the world. I propose to identify these resources by means of an Aristotelian concept, a linguistic concept (or, better yet, one pertaining to the art of rhetoric): the "common places," the *topoi koinoi*.

When we speak today of "common places," we mean, for the most part, stereotypical expressions, by now devoid of any meaning, banalities, lifeless metaphors ("morning is golden-mouthed"), trite linguistic conventions. Certainly this was not the original meaning of the expression "common places." For Aristotle (*Rhetoric*, I, 2, 1358a) the *topoi koinoi* are the most generally valid logical and linguistic forms of all of our discourse (let us even say, the skeletal structure of it); they allow for the existence of every individual expression we use and they give structure to these expressions as well. Such "places" are *common* because no one can do without them (from the refined orator to the drunkard who mumbles words hard to understand, from the business person to the politician). Aristotle points out three of these "places": the connection between more and less, the opposition of opposites, and the category of reciprocity ("If I am her brother, she is my sister").

These categories, like every true skeletal structure, never appear as such. They are the woof of the "life of the mind," but they are an *inconspicuous* woof. What is it, then, that can actually be seen in the forms of our discourse? The "special places," as Aristotle calls them (*topoi idioi*). These are ways of saying something—metaphors, witticisms, allocutions, etc.—which are appropriate in one or another sphere of associative life. "Special places" are ways of saying/thinking something which end up being appropriate at a local political party headquarters, or in church, or in a university classroom, or among sports fans of a certain team. And so on. Whether it be the life of the city or its *ethos* (shared customs), these are articulated by means of "special places" which are different from one another and often incompatible. A certain expression might function in one situation and not in another; a certain type of argumentation might succeed in convincing one audience, but not another, etc.

The transformation with which we must come to terms can be summarized in this way: in today's world, the "special places" of discourse and of argumentation are perishing and dissolving, while immediate visibility is being gained by the "common places," or by generic logical-linguistic forms which establish the pattern for all forms of discourse. This means that in order to get a sense of orientation in the world and to protect ourselves from its dangers, we can not rely on those forms of thought, of reasoning, or of discourse which have their niche in one particular context or another. The clan of sports fans, the religious community, the branch of a political party, the workplace: all of these "places" obviously continue to exist, but none of them is sufficiently characterized or characterizing as to be able to offer us a wind rose, or a standard of orientation, a trustworthy compass, a unity of specific customs, of specific ways of saying/ thinking things. Everywhere, and in every situation, we speak/ think in the same way, on the basis of logical-linguistic constructs which are as fundamental as they are broadly general. An ethical-rhetorical topography is disappearing. The "common places" (these inadequate principles of the "life of the mind") are moving to the forefront: the connection between more and less, the opposition of opposites, the relationship of reciprocity, etc. These "common places," and these alone, are what exist in terms of offering us a standard of orientation, and thus, some sort of refuge from the direction in which the world is going.

Being no longer inconspicuous, but rather having been flung into the forefront, the "common places" are the apotropaic resource of the contemporary multitude. They appear on the surface, like a toolbox containing things which are immediately useful. What else are they, these "common places," if not the fundamental core of the "life of the mind," the epicenter of that linguistic (in the strictest sense of the word) animal which is the human animal?

Thus, we could say that the "life of the mind" becomes, in itself, *public*. We turn to the most general categories in order to equip ourselves for the most varied specific situations, no longer having at our disposal any "special" or sectorial ethical-communicative codes. The feeling of not-feeling-at-home and the preeminence of the "common places" go hand in hand. The intellect as such, the pure intellect, becomes the concrete compass wherever the substantial communities fail, and we are always exposed to the world in its totality. The intellect, even in its most rarefied functions, is presented as something *common* and conspicuous. The "common places" are no longer an unnoticed background, they are no longer concealed by the springing forth of "special places." The "life of the mind" is the One which lies beneath the mode of being of the multitude. Let me repeat, and I must insist upon this: the movement to the forefront on the part of the intellect as such, the fact that the most general and abstract linguistic structures are becoming instruments for orienting one's own conduct—this situation, in my opinion, is one of the conditions which define the contemporary multitude.

A short while ago I spoke of the "public intellect." But the expression "public intellect" contradicts a long tradition according to which thought would be understood as a secluded and solitary activity, one which separates us from our peers, an interior action, devoid of visual manifestations, outside of the handling of human affairs. It seems that only one thinker takes exception to this long tradition according to which the "life of the mind" is resistant to publicness; in several pages of Marx we see the intellect being presented as something exterior and collective, as a public good. In the "Fragment on Machines" of the *Grundrisse*, (Notebook VII) Marx speaks of a *general intellect*: he uses these words in English to give emphasis to the expression, as though he wanted to place them in italics. The notion of "general intellect" can derive from several sources: perhaps it is a polemical response to the "general will" of Rousseau (the intellect, not the will, according to Marx, is that which joins together those who bring about production); or perhaps the "general intellect" is the materialistic renewal of the Aristotelian concept of *nous poietikos* (the productive, poietic intellect). But philology is not what matters here. What matters is the exterior, collective, social character which belongs to intellectual activity when this activity becomes, according to Marx, the true mainspring of the production of wealth.

With the exception of these pages in Marx, I repeat, tradition has attributed to the intellect those characteristics which illustrate its insensitivity to, and estrangement from, the public sphere. In one of the youthful writings of Aristotle, the *Protrepticus*, the life of the thinker is compared to the life of the stranger. Thinkers must live estranged from their community, must distance themselves from the buzzing activity of the multitude, must mute the sounds of the agora. With respect to public life, to the political-social community, thinkers and strangers alike do not feel themselves, in the strict sense of the expression, to be at home. This is a good point of departure for focusing on the condition of the contemporary multitude. But it is a good point of departure only if we agree to draw some other conclusions from the analogy between the stranger and the thinker.

Being a stranger, that is to say "not-feeling-at-home," is today a condition common to many, an inescapable and shared condition. So then, those who do not feel at home, in order to get a sense of orientation and to protect themselves, must turn to the "common places," or to the most general categories of the linguistic intellect; in this sense, strangers are always thinkers. As you see, I am inverting the direction of the analogy: it is not the thinkers who become strangers in the eyes of the community to which the thinkers belong, but the strangers, the multitude of those "with no home," who are absolutely obliged to attain the *status* of thinkers. Those "without a home" have no choice but to behave like thinkers: not in order for them to learn something about biology or advanced mathematics, but because they turn to the most essential categories of the abstract intellect in order to protect themselves from the blows of random chance, in order to take refuge from contingency and from the unforeseen.

In Aristotle, the thinker is the stranger, yes, but only provisionally: once he has finished writing the *Metaphysics*, he can return to the task of dealing with common affairs. In the same way, even the strangers in the strict sense of the word, the Spartans who have come to Athens, are strangers for a specific amount of time: sooner or later, they will be able to return to their country. For the contemporary multitude, instead, the condition of "not feeling at home" is permanent and irreversible. The absence of a substantial community and of any connected "special places" makes it such that the life of the stranger, the not-feeling-at-home, the *bios xenikos*, are unavoidable and lasting experiences. The multitude of those "without a home" places its trust in the intellect, in the "common places:" in its own way, then, it is a multitude of thinkers (even if these thinkers have only an elementary school education and never read a book, not even under torture).

And now a secondary observation. Sometimes we speak about the *childishness* of contemporary metropolitan forms of behavior. We speak about it in a deprecatory tone. Once we have agreed that such deprecation is foolish, it would be worth it to ask ourselves if there is something of consistency (in short, a kernel of truth) in the connection between metropolitan life and childhood. Perhaps childhood is the ontogenetic matrix of every subsequent search for protection from the blows of the surrounding world; it exemplifies the necessity of conquering a constituent sense of indecision, an original uncertainty (indecision and uncertainty which at times give way to shame, a feeling unknown to the non-human "baby" which knows from the beginning how to behave). The human baby protects itself by means of *repetition* (the same fairy tale, one more time, or the same game, or the same gesture). Repetition is understood as a protective strategy in the face of the shock caused by new and unexpected experiences. So, the problem looks like this: is it not true that the experience of the baby is transferred into adult experience, into the prevalent forms of behavior at the center of the great urban aggregates (described by Simmel, Benjamin, and so many others)? The childhood experience of repetition is prolonged even into adulthood, since it constitutes the principal form of safe haven in the absence of solidly established customs, of substantial communities, of a developed and complete *ethos*. In traditional societies (or, if you like, in the experience of the "people"), the repetition which is so dear to babies gave way to more complex and articulated forms of protection: to *ethos*; that is to say, to the usages and customs, to the habits which constitute the base of the substantial communities. Now, in the age of the multitude, this substitution no longer occurs. Repetition, far from being replaced, persists. It was Walter Benjamin who got the point. He dedicated a great deal of attention to childhood, to childish games, to the love which a baby has for repetition; and together with this, he identified the sphere in which new forms of perception are created with the technical reproducibility of a work of art (Benjamin, *Illuminations*). So then, there is something to believe in the idea that there is a connection between these two facets of thought. Within the possibility of technical reproduction, the child's request for "one more time" comes back again, strengthened; or we might say that the need for repetition as a form of refuge surfaces again. The publicness of the mind, the conspicuousness of "common places," the *general intellect*—these are also manifested as forms of the reassuring nature of repetition. It is true: today's multitude has something childish in it: but this something is as serious as can be.

Publicness without a public sphere

We have said that the multitude is defined by the feeling of not-feeling-at-home, just as it was defined by the consequent familiarity with "common places," with the abstract intellect. We need to add, now, that the dialectic dread-safe haven is rooted precisely in this familiarity with the abstract intellect. The public and shared character of the "life of the mind" is colored with ambivalence: it is also, in and of itself, the host to negative possibilities, to formidable figures. The public intellect is the unifying base from which there can spring forth either forms of ghastly protection or forms of protection capable of achieving a real sense of comfort (according to the degree in which, as we have said, they safeguard us from the former forms of protection). The public intellect which the multitude draws upon is the point of departure for opposing developments. When the fundamental abilities of the human being (thought, language, self-reflection, the capacity for learning) come to the forefront, the situation can take on a disquieting and oppressive appearance; or it can even give way to a non-public public sphere, to a *non-governmental* public sphere, far from the myths and rituals of sovereignty.

My thesis, in extremely concise form, is this: if the publicness of the intellect does not yield to the realm of a public sphere, of a political space in which the many can tend to common affairs, then it produces terrifying effects. *A publicness without a public sphere*: here is the negative side—the evil, if you wish—of the experience of the multitude. Freud in the essay "The Uncanny" (Freud, *Collected Papers*) shows how the extrinsic power of thought can take on anguishing features. He says that people who are ill, for whom thoughts have an exterior, practical and immediately operative power, fear becoming conditioned and overwhelmed by others. It is the same situation, moreover, which is brought about in a spiritualist séance in which the participants are bound together in a fused relationship which seems to nullify every trace of individual identity. So then, the belief in the "omnipotence of thought," studied by Freud, and the extreme situation of the spiritualist séance exemplify clearly what *publicness without a public sphere* can become; what *general intellect* can become when it is not articulated within a political space.

The *general intellect*, or public intellect, if it does not become a *republic*, a public sphere, a political community, drastically increases forms of submission. To make the point clear, let us think about contemporary production. The *sharing* of linguistic and cognitive habits is the constituent element of the post-Fordist process of labor. All the workers enter into production in as much as they are speaking-thinking. This has nothing to do, mind you, with "professionality" or with the ancient concept of "skill" or "craftsmanship": to speak/to think are generic habits of the human animal, the opposite of any sort of specialization. This preliminary *sharing* in one way characterizes the "many," seen as being "many," the multitude; in another way, it is itself the base of today's production. *Sharing*, in so far as it is a technical requirement, is opposed to the *division* of labor—it contradicts that division and causes it to crumble. Of course this does not mean that work loads are no longer subdivided, parceled out, etc.; rather, it means that the segmentation of duties no longer answers to objective "technical" criteria, but is, instead, explicitly arbitrary, reversible, changeable. As far as capital is concerned, what really counts is the original sharing of linguistic-cognitive talents, since it is this sharing which guarantees readiness, adaptability, etc., in reacting to innovation. So, it is evident that this sharing of generic cognitive and linguistic talents within the process of real production does not become a public sphere, does not become a political community or a constitutional principle. So then, what happens?

The publicness of the intellect, that is to say the sharing of the intellect, in one sense causes every rigid division of labor to fall flat on its back; in another sense, however, it fosters *personal dependence. General intellect,* the end of the division of labor, personal dependency: the three facets are interrelated. The publicness of the intellect, when it does not take place in a public sphere, translates into an *unchecked proliferation of hierarchies* as groundless as they are thriving. The dependency is *personal* in two senses of the word: in the world of labor one depends on this person or on that person, not on rules endowed with anonymous coercive power; moreover, it is the whole person who is subdued, the person's basic communicative and cognitive habits.

Which One for the Many?

The point of departure for our analysis was the opposition between the terms "people" and "multitude." From what we have discussed up to this point, it remains clear that the multitude does not rid itself of the *One*, of the universal, of the common/shared; rather, it redefines the One. The One of the multitude no longer has anything to do with the One constituted by the State, with the One towards which the people converge.

The people are the result of a centripetal movement: from atomized individuals, to the unity of the "body politic," to sovereignty. The extreme outcome of this centripetal movement is the One. The multitude, on the other hand, is the outcome of a centrifugal movement: from the One to the Many. But which One is it that serves as the starting point from which the many differentiate themselves and remain so? Certainly it can not be the State; it must have to do with some completely different form of unity/universality. We can now consider once again a point to which we referred at the beginning of our analysis.

The unity which the multitude has behind itself is constituted by the "common places" of the mind, by the linguistic-cognitive faculties common to the species, by the *general intellect.* It has to do with a unity/universality which is visibly unlike that of the state. Let us be clear: the cognitive-linguistic habits of the species do not come to the forefront because someone decides to make them come to the forefront; they do so out of necessity, or because they constitute a form of protection in a society devoid of substantial communities (or of "special places").

The One of the multitude, then, is not the One of the people. The multitude does not converge into a *volonté générale* for one simple reason: because it already has access to a *general intellect.* The public intellect, however, which appears in the post-Ford world as a mere resource of production, can constitute a different "constitutional principle"; it can overshadow a *non-state public sphere.* The many, in as much as they are many, use the publicness of the intellect as their base or pedestal: for better or for worse.

Certainly there is a substantial difference between the contemporary multitude and the multitude which was studied by seventeenth century philosophers of political thought. At the dawning of the modern era, the "many" coincided with the citizens of the communal republics prior to the birth of the great national States. Those "many" made use of the "right of resistance," of the *jus resistentiae.* That right, nonsensically, does not mean legitimate defense: it is something more subtle and complicated. The "right of resistance" consists of validating the prerogatives of an individual or of a local community, or of a corporation, in contrast to the central power structure, thus safeguarding forms of life which have *already* been affirmed as free-standing forms, thus protecting practices *already* rooted in society. It means, then, defending something positive: it is a *conservative* violence (in the good and noble sense of the word.) Perhaps the *jus resistentiae* (or the right to protect something which is already in place and is worthy of continuing to exist) is what provides the strongest connection between the seventeenth century *multitudo* and the post-Ford multitude. Even for the latter "multitude," it is not a question of "seizing power," of constructing a new State or a new monopoly of political decision making; rather, it has to do with defending plural experiences, forms of non-representative democracy, of non-governmental usages and customs. As far as the rest is concerned, it is difficult not to see the differences between the two "multitudes": the contemporary multitude is fundamentally based upon the presumption of a One which is more, not less, universal than the State: public intellect, language, "common places" (just think, if you will, about the World-wide Web…). Furthermore, the contemporary multitude carries with it the history of capitalism and is closely bound to the needs of the labor class.

We must hold at bay the demon of the analogy, the short circuiting between the ancient and the very modern; we need to delineate in high relief the original historical traits of the contemporary multitude, while avoiding to define this multitude as simply a remake of something which once was. Let me give an example. It is typical of the post-Ford multitude to foment the collapse of political representation: not as an anarchic gesture, but as a means of calmly and realistically searching for new political forms. Of course Hobbes was already putting us on alert with reference to the tendency of the multitude to take on the forms of irregular political organisms: "in their nature but leagues, or sometimes mere concourse of people, without union to any particular design, not by obligation of one to another" (Hobbes, *Leviathan*: 154). But it is obvious that non-representative democracy based upon the *general intellect* has an entirely different significance: it is in no way interstitial, marginal or residual; rather, it is the concrete appropriation and re-articulation of the knowledge/power unity which has congealed within the administrative modern machine of the States.

When we speak of "multitude," we run up against a complex problem: we must confront a concept without a history, without a lexicon, whereas the concept of "people" is a completely codified concept for which we have appropriate words and nuances of every sort. This is obviously the way it is. I have already said that the "people" prevailed against the "multitude" in the political-philosophical thought of the seventeenth century: thus, the "people" have enjoyed the privilege of a suitable lexicon. With regard to the multitude, we are left, instead, with the absolute lack of codification, with the absence of a clear conceptual vocabulary. But this is a wonderful challenge for philosophers and sociologists, above all for doing research in the field. It involves working on concrete matters, examining them in detail, but, at the same time deriving theoretical categories from them. There is a dual movement here, from things to words, and from words to things: this requires the post-Ford multitude. And it is, I repeat, an exciting task.

It is quite clear that "people" and "multitude" are two categories which are more in line with political thought than with sociology; in fact, they signify, between themselves, alternate forms of political existence. But it is my opinion that the notion of the multitude is extraordinarily rich in terms of allowing us to understand, to assess the modes of being of post-Ford subordinate labor, to understand some of the forms of behavior of that labor which at first sight seemed so enigmatic. As I will try to explain more completely in the second day of our symposium, this is precisely a category of political thought which, having been defeated in the theoretical debate of its time, now presents itself again as a most valuable instrument for the analysis of living labor in the post-Ford era. Let us say that the multitude is an amphibian category: on one hand it speaks to us of social production based on knowledge and language; on the other hand, it speaks of the crisis of the form-of-State. And perhaps there is a strong connection between these two things. Carl Schmitt is someone who has grasped the essential nature of the State and who is the major theoretician of the politics of the past century; in the Sixties, when he was already an old man, he wrote a very bitter (for him) statement, the sense of which is that as the multitude reappears, the people fade away: "The era of stateness [*Staatlichkeit*] is nearing its end [...]. The State as the model of political unity, the State as the holder of the most extraordinary of all monopolies, that is to say, of the monopoly of political decision-making [...] is being dethroned" (Schmitt, *Der Begriff*: 10 [note: English translation from the German, by the translators]). One important addition, however, must be made: this monopoly of decision making can be truly taken away from the State only when it ceases for once and for all to be a monopoly, only when the multitude asserts its centrifugal character.

I would like to conclude this first day of our seminar by dispelling, as much as I can, a misunderstanding into which it is easy to fall. It might seem as though the multitude would mark the end of the labor class. In the universe of the "many," there is no longer room for the blue collar workers, all of them equal, who make up a unified body among them, a body which is not very sensitive to the kaleidoscope of the "difference" among them.

This is a foolish way of thinking, one which is dear to those who feel the need to oversimplify questions, to get high on words meant for effect (to produce electroshocks for monkeys, as a friend of mine used to say). Neither in Marx, nor in the opinion of any serious person, is labor class equated with certain habits, with certain usages and customs, etc. The labor class is a theoretical concept, not a snap-shot photograph kept as a souvenir: it signifies the subject which produces relative and absolute surplus value. So then, the contemporary working class, the current subordinate labor-power and its cognitive-linguistic collaboration, bear the traits of the multitude, rather than of the people. However, this multitude no longer assumes the "popular" vocation to stateness [*statualità*]. The notion of "multitude" does not overturn the concept of the working class, since this concept was not bound by definition to that of "people." Being "multitude" does not interfere at all with producing surplus value. Since the labor class no longer assumes the mode of being of the people, but rather, that of the multitude, many things change, of course: the mentality, the forms of organization and of conflict. Everything becomes complicated. How much easier it would be to say that there is a multitude now, that there is no more labor class ... But if we really want simplicity at all costs, all we have to do is drink up a bottle of red wine.

On the other hand, there are passages even in Marx in which the labor class loses the appearance of the "people" and acquires the features of the "multitude." Just one example: let us think about the pages of the last chapter of the first book of the *Capital*, where Marx analyzes the condition of the labor class in the United States (Volume 1, Chap. 33, "The modern theory of colonization"). There is, in that chapter, some great writing on the subject of the American West, on the exodus from the East, on the individual initiative of the "many." The European laborers, driven away from their own countries by epidemics, famines and economic crises, go off to work on the East Coast of the United States. But let us note: they remain there for a few years, *only* for a few years. Then they desert the factory, moving West, towards free lands. Wage labor is seen as a transitory phase, rather than as a life sentence. Even if only for a twenty-year period, the wage laborers had the possibility of planting the seeds of disorder into the ironclad laws of the labor market: by renouncing their own initial condition, they brought about a relative shortage of manpower and thus a raise in salaries. Marx, in describing this situation, offers us a very vivid portrait of a labor class which is also a multitude.

Labor, Action, Intellect

Day Two

In our previous seminar I tried to illustrate the mode of being of the multitude, beginning with the dialectic dread-safe haven. Today, I would like to discuss the classical division of human experience into three fundamental spheres: Labor (or poiesis), political Action (or praxis) and Intellect (or life of the mind). The goal here is still the same: to articulate and to investigate in depth the notion of multitude.

As you will recall, "multitude" is a central category of political thought: it is called into question here in order to explain some of the salient features of the post-Ford mode of production. We do so on the condition that we understand "mode of production" to mean not only one particular economic configuration, but also a composite unity of forms of life, a social, anthropological and ethical cluster: "ethical," let us note, and not "moral"; in question here are common practices, usages and customs, not the dimension of the must-be. So then, I would like to maintain that the contemporary multitude has as its background the crisis of the subdivision of human experience into Labor, (political) Action and Intellect. The multitude affirms itself, in high relief, as a mode of being in which there is a juxtaposition, or at least a hybridization, between spheres which, until very recently, even during the Ford era, seemed clearly distinct and separated.

Labor, Action, Intellect: in the style of a tradition which goes back to Aristotle and which has been revisited with particular efficacy and passion by Hannah Arendt (Arendt, *The Human Condition*), this tripartitioning has seemed clear, realistic, nearly unquestionable. It has put down solid roots in the realm of common sense: it is not a question, then, of an undertaking which is only philosophical, but of a widely shared pattern of thought. When I began to get involved in politics, in the Sixties, I considered this subdivision to be something indisputable; it seemed to me as unquestionable as any immediate tactile or visual perception. It was not necessary to have read Aristotle's *Nicomachean Ethics* to know that labor, political action, and intellectual reflection constituted three spheres supported by radically heterogeneous principles and criteria. Obviously, this heterogeneity did not exclude intersection: political reflection could be applied to politics; in turn, political action was often, and willingly, nourished by themes related to the sphere of production, etc. But, as numerous as the intersections were, Labor, Intellect, and Politics remained essentially distinct. For structural reasons.

Labor is the organic exchange with nature, the production of new objects, a repetitive and foreseeable process. The pure intellect has a solitary and inconspicuous character: the meditation of the thinker escapes the notice of others; theoretical reflection mutes the world of appearances. Differently from Labor, political Action comes between social relations, not between natural materials; it has to do with the possible and the unforeseen; it does not obstruct, with ulterior motives, the context in which it operates; rather, it modifies this very context. Differently from the Intellect, political Action is public, consigned to exteriority, to contingency, to the buzzing of the "many;" it involves, to use the words of Hannah, "the presence of others" (*Human Condition*, Chap. V, "Action"). The concept of political Action can be deduced by opposition with respect to the other two spheres.

So then, this ancient tripartitioning, which was still encysted into the realm of common sense of the generation which made its appearance in the public scene in the Sixties, is exactly what has failed today. That is to say, the boundaries between pure intellectual activity, political action, and labor have dissolved. I will maintain, in particular, that the world of so-called post-Fordist labor has absorbed into itself many of the typical characteristics of political action; and that this fusion between Politics and Labor constitutes a decisive physiognomic trait of the contemporary multitude.

Juxtaposition of poiesis and praxis

Contemporary labor has introjected into itself many characteristics which originally marked the experience of politics. *Poiesis* has taken on numerous aspects of *praxis*. This is the first aspect of the most general form of hybridization which I would like to address.

But let us note that even Hannah Arendt insisted on denouncing the collapse of the border between labor and politics—whereby politics does not mean life in some local party headquarters, but the generically human experience of beginning something again, an intimate relationship with contingency and the unforeseen, being in the presence of others. Politics, according to Arendt, has taken to imitating labor. The politics of the twentieth century, in her judgment, has become a sort of fabrication of new objects: the State, the political party, history, etc. So then, I maintain that things have gone in the opposite direction from what Arendt seems to believe: it is not that politics has conformed to labor; it is rather that labor has acquired the traditional features of political action. My reasoning is opposite and symmetrical with respect to that of Arendt. I maintain that it is in the world of contemporary labor that we find the "being in the presence of others," the relationship with the presence of others, the beginning of new processes, and the constitutive familiarity with contingency, the unforeseen and the possible. I maintain that post-Fordist labor, the productive labor of surplus, subordinate labor, brings into play the talents and the qualifications which, according to a secular tradition, had more to do with political action.

Incidentally, this explains, in my opinion, the crisis of politics, the sense of scorn surrounding political praxis today, the disrepute into which action has fallen. In fact, political action now seems, in a disastrous way, like some superfluous duplication of the experience of labor, since the latter experience, even if in a deformed and despotic manner, has subsumed into itself certain structural characteristics of political action. The sphere of politics, in the strictest sense of the word, follows closely the procedures and stylistic elements which define the current state of labor; but let us note: it follows them closely while offering a poorer, cruder and more simplistic version of these procedures and stylistic elements. Politics offers a network of communication and a cognitive content of a more wretched variety than what is carried out in the current productive process. While less complex than labor and yet too similar to it, political action seems, all the same, like something not very desirable at all.

The inclusion of certain structural features of political praxis in contemporary production helps us to understand why the post-Ford multitude might be seen, today, as a *de-politicized* multitude. There is already too much politics in the world of wage labor (*in as much as it is* wage labor) in order for politics as such to continue to enjoy an autonomous dignity.

On virtuosity. From Aristotle to Glenn Gould

The subsumption into the labor process of what formerly guaranteed an indisputable physiognomy for public Action can be clarified by means of an ancient, but by no means ineffective, category: *virtuosity.*

Accepting, for now, the normal meaning of the word, by "virtuosity" I mean the special capabilities of a performing artist. A virtuoso, for example, is the pianist who offers us a memorable performance of Schubert; or it is a skilled dancer, or a persuasive orator, or a teacher who is never boring, or a priest who delivers a fascinating sermon. Let us consider carefully what defines the activity of virtuosos, of performing artists. First of all, theirs is *an activity which finds its own fulfillment (that is, its own purpose) in itself,* without objectifying itself into an end product, without settling into a "finished product," or into an object which would survive the performance. Secondly, it is *an activity which requires the presence of others,* which exists only in the presence of an audience.

An activity without an end product: the performance of a pianist or of a dancer does not leave us with a defined object distinguishable from the performance itself, capable of continuing after the performance has ended. An activity which requires the presence of others: the *performance* [Author uses the English word here] makes sense only if it is seen or heard. It is obvious that these two characteristics are inter-related: virtuosos need the presence of an audience precisely because they are not producing an end product, an object which will circulate through the world once the activity has ceased. Lacking a specific extrinsic product, the virtuoso has to rely on witnesses.

The category of virtuosity is discussed in the *Nicomachean Ethics*; it appears here and there in modern political thought, even in the twentieth century; it even holds a small place in Marx's criticism of political economics. In the *Nicomachean Ethics* Aristotle distinguishes labor (or poiesis) from political action (or praxis), utilizing precisely the notion of virtuosity: we have labor when an object is produced, an opus which can be separated from action; we have praxis when the purpose of action is found in action itself. Aristotle writes: "For while making has an end other than itself, action cannot; for good action [understood both as ethical conduct and as political action, Virno adds] itself is its end" (*Nicomachean Ethics*, VI, 1140 b). Implicitly resuming Aristotle's idea, Hannah Arendt compares the performing artists, the virtuosos, to those who are engaged in political action. She writes: "The performing arts [...] have indeed a strong affinity with politics. Performing artists—dancers, play-actors, musicians, and the like—need an audience to show their virtuosity, just as acting men need the presence of others before whom they can appear; both need a publicly organized space for their 'work,' and both depend upon others for the performance itself" (Arendt, *Between Past and Future*: 154).

One could say that every political action is *virtuosic*. Every political action, in fact, shares with virtuosity a sense of contingency, the absence of a "finished product," the immediate and unavoidable presence of others. On the one hand, all virtuosity is intrinsically *political*. Think about the case of Glenn Gould (Gould, *The Glenn Gould Reader*; and Schneider, *Glenn Gould*). This great pianist paradoxically, hated the distinctive characteristics of his activity as a performing artist; to put it another way, he detested public exhibition. Throughout his life he fought against the "political dimension" intrinsic to his profession. At a certain point Gould declared that he wanted to abandon the "*active life*," that is, the act of being exposed to the eyes of others (note: "*active life*" is the traditional name for politics). In order to make his own virtuosity non-political, he sought to bring his activity as a performing artist as close as possible to the idea of labor, in the strictest sense, which leaves behind extrinsic products. This meant closing himself inside a recording studio, passing off the production of records (excellent ones, by the way) as an "end product." In order to avoid the public-political dimension ingrained in virtuosity, he had to pretend that his masterly performances produced a defined object (independent of the performance itself). Where there is an end product, an autonomous product, there is labor, no longer virtuosity, nor, *for that reason*, politics.

Even Marx speaks of pianists, orators, dancers, etc. He speaks of them in some of his most important writings: in his "Results of the Immediate Process of Production," and then, in almost identical terms, in his *Theories of Surplus-value*. Marx analyzes intellectual labor, distinguishing between its two principal types. On one hand, there is immaterial or mental activity which "results in commodities which exist separately from the producer [...] books, paintings and all products of art as distinct from the artistic achievement of the practicing artist" (in Appendix to *Capital, Vol. I*, "Results of the Immediate Process of Production": 1048). This is the first type of intellectual labor. On the other hand, Marx writes, we need to consider all those activities in which the "product is not separable from the act of producing" (ibid., 1048)—those activities, that is, which find in themselves their own fulfillment without being objectivized into an end product which might surpass them. This is the same distinction which Aristotle made between material production and political action. The only difference is that Marx in this instance is not concerned with political action; rather, he is analyzing two different representations of labor. To these specifically defined types of poiesis he applies the distinction between activity-with-end-product and activity-without-end-product. The second type of intellectual labor (activities in which "product is not separable from the act of producing,") includes, according to Marx, all those whose labor turns into a virtuosic performance: pianists, butlers, dancers, teachers, orators, medical doctors, priests, etc.

So then, if intellectual labor which produces an end product does not pose any special problems, labor without an end product (virtuosic labor) places Marx in an embarrassing situation. The first type of intellectual labor conforms to the definition of "productive labor." But what about the second type? I remember in passing, that for Marx, productive labor is not subordinate or fatiguing or menial labor, but is precisely and only that kind of labor which produces surplus-value. Of course, even virtuosic performances can, in principle, produce surplus-value: the activity of the dancer, of the pianist, etc., if organized in a capitalistic fashion, can be a source of profit. But Marx is disturbed by the strong resemblance between the activity of the performing artist and the *servile* duties which, thankless and frustrating as they are, do not produce surplus value, and thus return to the realm of non-productive labor. Servile labor is that labor in which no *capital* is invested, but a wage is paid (example: the personal services of a butler). According to Marx, even if the "virtuosist" workers represent, on one hand, a not very significant exception to the quantitative point of view, on the other hand, and this is what counts more, they almost always converge into the realm of servile/non-productive labor. Such convergence is sanctioned precisely by the fact that their activity does not give way to an independent end product: where an autonomous finished product is lacking, for the most part one cannot speak of productive (surplus-value) labor. Marx virtually accepts the equation work-without-end-product = personal services. In conclusion, virtuosic labor, for Marx, is a form of wage labor which is not, at the same time, productive labor (*Theories of Surplus-value*: 410–411).

Let us try to sum things up. Virtuosity is open to two alternatives: either it conceals the structural characteristics of political activity (lack of an end product, being exposed to the presence of others, sense of contingency, etc.), as Aristotle and Hannah Arendt suggest; or, as in Marx, it takes on the features of "wage labor which is not productive labor." This bifurcation decays and falls to pieces when *productive* labor, in its totality, appropriates the special characteristics of the performing artist. In post-

Fordism, those who produce surplus-value behave—from the structural point of view, of course—like the pianists, the dancers, etc., and *for this reason*, like the politicians. With reference to contemporary production, Hannah Arendt's observation on the activity of the performing artist and the politician rings clear: in order to work, one needs a "publicly organized space." In post-Fordism, Labor requires a " publicly organized space" and resembles a virtuosic performance (without end product). This publicly organized space is called "cooperation" by Marx. One could say: at a certain level in the development of productive social forces, labor cooperation introjects verbal communication into itself, or, more precisely, a complex of *political actions*.

Do you remember the extremely renowned commentary of Max Weber on politics as profession? (Weber, *Politics as a Vocation*) Weber elaborates on a series of qualities which define the politician: knowing how to place the health of one's own soul in danger; an equal balance between the ethics of convincing and the ethics of responsibility; dedication to one's goal, etc. We should re-read this text with reference to Toyotaism, to labor based upon language, to the productive mobilization of the cognitive faculties. Weber's wisdom speaks to us of the qualities required today for material production.

The speaker as performing artist

Each one of us is, and has always been, a virtuoso, a performing artist, at times mediocre or awkward, but, in any event, a virtuoso. In fact, the fundamental model of virtuosity, the experience which is the base of the concept, is *the activity of the speaker*. This is not the activity of a knowledgeable and erudite locutor, but of *any* locutor. Human verbal language, not being a pure tool or a complex of instrumental signals (these are characteristics which are inherent, if anything, in the languages of non-human animals: one need only think of bees and of the signals which they use for coordinating the procurement of food), has its fulfillment in itself and does not produce (at least not as a rule, not necessarily) an "object" independent of the very act of having been uttered.

Language is "without end product." Every utterance is a virtuosic performance. And this is so, also because, obviously, utterance is connected (directly or indirectly) to the presence of others. Language presupposes and, at the same time, institutes once again the "publicly organized space" which Arendt speaks about. One would need to reread the passages from the *Nicomachean Ethics* on the essential difference between poiesis (production) and praxis (politics) with very close connection to the notion of *parole* in Saussure (Saussure, *Course*) and, above all, to the analyses of Emile Benveniste (Benveniste, *Problems*) on the subject of utterance (where "utterance" is not understood to mean the content of what is uttered, that "which is said," but the interjection of a word as such, the very fact of speaking). In this way one would establish that the differential characteristics of praxis with respect to poiesis coincide absolutely with the differential characteristics of verbal language with respect to motility or even to non-verbal communication.

There is more to the story. The speaker alone—unlike the pianist, the dancer or the actor—can do without a script or a score. The speaker's virtuosity is twofold: not only does it not produce an end product which is distinguishable from performance, but it does not even leave behind an end product which could be actualized by means of performance. In fact, the act of *parole* makes use only of the *potentiality* of language, or better yet, of the generic faculty of language: not of a pre-established text in detail. The virtuosity of the speaker is the prototype and apex of all other forms of virtuosity, precisely because it includes within itself the potential/act relationship, whereas ordinary or derivative virtuosity, instead, presupposes a determined act (as in Bach's *"Goldberg" Variations*, let us say), which can be relived over and over again. But I will return to this point later.

It is enough to say, for now, that contemporary production becomes "virtuosic" (and thus political) precisely because it includes within itself linguistic experience as such. If this is so, the matrix of post-Fordism can be found in the industrial sectors in which there is "production of communication by means of communication"; hence, in the culture industry.

Culture industry: anticipation and paradigm

Virtuosity becomes labor for the masses with the onset of a culture industry. It is here that the virtuoso begins to punch a time card. Within the sphere of a culture industry, in fact, activity without an end product, that is to say, communicative activity which has itself as an end, is a distinctive, central and necessary element. But, exactly for this reason, it is above all within the culture industry that the structure of wage labor has overlapped with that of political action.

Within the sectors where communication is produced by means of communication, responsibilities and roles are, at the same time, "virtuosic" and "political." In his most important novel, *La vita agra* [*Bitter*

Life], a distinguished Italian writer, Luciano Bianciardi, describes the splendors and miseries of the culture industry in Milan during the Fifties. In one remarkable page of this book, he effectively illustrates what distinguishes culture industry from traditional industry and from agriculture. The protagonist of La *vita agra*, having arrived in Milan from Grosseto with the intention of avenging recent job related deaths that took place in his region, ends up becoming involved in the budding culture industry. After a brief time, however, he is fired. The following is a passage which, today, has unmistakable theoretical merit: "[...] And they fired me, only on account of the fact that I drag my feet, I move slowly, I look around even when it is not absolutely necessary. In our business, however, we need to lift our feet high off the ground, and bang them down again on the floor noisily, we need to move, hit the pavement, jump up, create dust, possibly a cloud of dust and then hide inside it. It is not like being a peasant or a worker. The peasant moves slowly because the work is so related to the seasons; the peasant cannot sow in July and harvest in February. Workers move quickly, but if they are on the assembly line, because on the line there are measured out periods of production, and if they do not move following that rhythm, they are in trouble [...]. But the fact is that the peasant belongs to the realm of primary activities and the worker to the realm of secondary activities. One produces something from nothing; the other transforms one thing into another. There is an easy measuring stick for the worker and for the peasant, one which is quantitative: does the factory produce so many pieces per hour, does the farm yield a profit? In our professions it is different, there are no quantitative measuring sticks. How does one measure the skill of a priest, or of a journalist, or of someone in public relations? *These people neither produce from scratch, nor transform.* They are neither primary nor secondary. Tertiary is what they are and what's more, I would dare say [...] even four times removed. They are neither instruments of production, nor drive belts of transmission. They are a lubricant, at the most pure Vaseline. How can one evaluate a priest, a journalist, a public relations person? How can one calculate the amount of faith, of purchasing desire, of likeability that these people have managed to muster up? No, we have no other yardstick in this case than the one which can measure one's capacity to float above water, and to ascend even higher, in short, to become a bishop. In other words, those who choose a tertiary or quaternary profession need *skills and aptitudes of a political kind.* Politics, as everybody knows has for a long time ceased to be the science of good government and has become, instead, the art of conquering and maintaining power. Therefore, the excellence of politicians is not measured according to the good that they manage to do for others, but is based on the swiftness with which they get to the top and on the amount of time they last there. [...] In the same way, in the tertiary and quaternary professions, *since there is no visible production of goods to function as a measuring stick*, the criterion will be the same" (Bianciardi, *La vita agra*: 129-32; Virno's italics [note: English translation from the original Italian by the translators]).

In many ways, Bianciardi's analysis is clearly dated, since it presents the functions of the culture industry as a marginal and outlandish exception to the rule. Moreover, it is at best superficial to reduce politics to a pure and simple overthrowing of power. In spite of this, the passage which I have just read shows exceptional intuition. In its own way, this intuition recalls and rehashes Arendt's thesis on the similarity between virtuosos and politicians, as well as Marx's notations about labor which does not have a separate "end product" as its goal. Bianciardi underscores the emerging "political dimension" of labor within the culture industry. But, and this is crucial, he links this dimension to the fact that in the culture industry there is no production of labor independent from activity itself. Where an extrinsic "end product" is lacking, there lies the ground for political action. I should clarify: in the culture industry (as is the case, after all, today in the post-Ford era for industry in general) the finished products which can be sold at the end of the productive process are surely not scarce. The crucial point is, though, that while the material production of objects is delegated to an automated system of machines, the services rendered by living labor, instead, resemble linguistic-virtuosic services more and more.

We should ask ourselves what role the culture industry assumed with relation to overcoming the Ford / Taylor model. I believe that it fine-tuned the paradigm of post-Fordist production on the whole. I believe therefore, that the mode of action of the culture industry became, from a certain point on, exemplary and pervasive. Within the culture industry, even in its archaic incarnation examined by Benjamin and Adorno, one can grasp early signs of a mode of production which later, in the post-Ford era, becomes generalized and elevated to the rank of *canon*.

To clarify, let us return, for a moment, to the critique of the communication industry leveled by the thinkers of the Frankfurt School. In the *Dialectic of Enlightenment* (Adorno and Horckheimer: 120–167) the authors maintain, roughly, that the "factories of the soul" (publishing, cinema, radio, television etc.) also conform to the Fordist criteria of serialization and parcelization. In those factories, also, the conveyer belt, the dominant symbol of automobile factories, seems to assert itself. Capitalism—this is the thesis—shows that it can mechanize and parcelize even its spiritual production, exactly as it has done with agriculture and the processing of metals. Serialization, insignificance of individual tasks, the econometrics of feelings: these are the recurrent *refrains*. Evidently, this critical approach allowed, in the peculiar case of the culture industry, for the continuation of some elements which resist a complete assimilation to the Fordist organization of the labor process. In the culture industry, that is to say, it was therefore necessary to maintain a certain space that was informal, not programmed, one which was open to the unforeseen spark, to communicative and creative improvisation: not in order to favor human creativity, naturally, but in order to achieve satisfactory levels of corporate productivity. However, for the Frankfurt School, these aspects were nothing but un-influential remnants, remains of the past, waste. What counted was the general Fordization of the culture industry. Now, it seems to me, from our present perspective, that it is not difficult to recognize that these purported remnants (with a certain space granted to the informal, to the unexpected, to the "unplanned") were, after all, loaded with future possibilities.

These were not remnants, but anticipatory omens. The informality of communicative behavior, the competitive interaction typical of a meeting, the abrupt diversion that can enliven a television program (in general, everything which it would have been dysfunctional to rigidify and regulate beyond a certain threshold), has become now, in the post-Ford era, a typical trait of the *entire* realm of social production. This is true not only for our contemporary culture industry, but also for Fiat in Melfi. If Bianciardi was discussing labor organized by a nexus between (virtuosic) activity-without-end-product and political attitudes as a marginal aberration, this has now become the rule. The intermingling of virtuosity, politics and labor has extended everywhere. What is left to question, if anything, is what specific role is carried out *today* by the communication industry, since all industrial sectors are inspired by its model. Has the very thing that once upon a time anticipated the post-Ford turning point become entirely unfolded? In order to answer this question, we should linger a while on the concept of "spectacle" and "society of the spectacle."

Language on the stage

I believe that the notion of "spectacle," though itself rather vague, provides a useful tool for deciphering some aspects of the post-Ford multitude (which is, in fact, a multitude of virtuosos, of workers who, in order to work, rely on generically "political" skills).

The concept of "spectacle," coined in the Sixties by the Situationists, is a truly theoretical concept, not foreign to the tenet of Marxian argumentation. According to Guy Debord "spectacle" is human communication which has become a commodity. What is delivered through the spectacle is precisely the human ability to communicate, verbal language as such. As we can see, the core of the issue is not a rancorous objection to consumer society (which is always slightly suspect, the risk being, as in the case of Pasolini, that of bemoaning the blessed cohabitation between low levels of consumerism and pellagra). Human communication, as spectacle, is a commodity among others, not outfitted with special qualities or prerogatives. On the other hand, it is a commodity which concerns, from a certain point on, all industrial sectors. This is where the problem lies.

On one hand, spectacle is the specific product of a specific industry, the so-called culture industry, in fact. On the other hand, in the post-Ford era, human communication is also an essential ingredient of productive cooperation in general; thus, it is the reigning productive force, something that goes beyond the domain of its own sphere, pertaining, instead, to the industry as a whole, to poiesis in its totality. In the spectacle we find exhibited, in a separate and fetishized form, the most relevant productive forces of society, those productive forces on which every contemporary work process must draw: linguistic competence, knowledge, imagination, etc. Thus, the spectacle has a *double nature*: a specific product of a particular industry, but also, at the same time, the quintessence of the mode of production in its entirety. Debord writes that the spectacle is "the general gloss on the rationality of the system." (Debord, ibid., Thesis 15) What presents the spectacle, so to speak, are the productive forces themselves of society as they overlap, in ever-greater measure, with linguistic-communicative competencies and with the *general intellect.*

The double nature of the spectacle is reminiscent, in some ways, of the double nature of money. As you know, money is a commodity among others, manufactured by the State Mint, in Rome, endowed of a metallic or paper form. But it also has a second nature: it is an equivalent, a unit of measurement, of all other commodities. Money is particular and universal at the same time; spectacle is particular and universal at the same time. This comparison, though without a doubt an attractive one, is incorrect. Unlike money, which measures the result of a productive process, one which has been concluded, spectacle concerns, instead, the productive process *in fieri*, in its unfolding, in its potential. The spectacle, according to Debord, reveals what women and men *can* do. While money mirrors in itself the value of commodities, thus showing what society has *already* produced, the spectacle exposes in a separate form that which the aggregate of society *can* be and do. If money is the "real abstraction" (to use a classic Marxian expression) which refers back to finished labor, to labor's past, according to Debord the spectacle is, instead, the "real abstraction" which portrays labor in itself, the present tense of labor. If money spearheads exchange, then the spectacle, human communication which has become a commodity, spearheads, if anything, productive communication. We must conclude, then, that the spectacle, which is human communicative capacity turned into commodity, does have a double nature which is different from that of money. But different in what way?

My hypothesis is that the communication industry (or rather, the spectacle, or even yet, the culture industry) is an industry among others, with its specific techniques, its particular procedures, its peculiar profits, etc.; on the other hand, it also plays the role of *industry of the means of production*. Traditionally, the industry of the means of production is the industry that produces machinery and other instruments to be used in the most varied sectors of production. However, in a situation in which the means of production are not reducible to machines but consist of linguistic-cognitive competencies inseparable from living labor, it is legitimate to assume that a conspicuous part of the so-called "means of production" consists of techniques and communicative procedures. Now, where are these techniques and procedures created, if not in the culture industry? The culture industry produces (regenerates, experiments with) communicative procedures, which are then destined to function also as means of production in the more traditional sectors of our contemporary economy. This is the role of the communication industry, once post-Fordism has become fully entrenched: an industry of the means of communication.

Virtuosity in the workplace

Virtuosity, with its intrinsic political dimension, not only characterizes the culture industry but the totality of contemporary social production. One could say that in the organization of labor in the post-Ford era, activity without an end product, previously a special and problematic case (one need only recall, in this regard, Marx's uncertainties), becomes the prototype of all wage labor. Let me repeat a point I made before: this does not mean that car dashboards are no longer produced but that, for an ever increasing numbers of professional tasks, the fulfillment of an action is internal to the action itself (that is, it does not consist of giving rise to an independent semi-labor).

A situation of this kind is foreshadowed by Marx himself in the *Grundrisse*, when he writes that with the advent of large, automated industry and the intensive and systematic application of the natural sciences to the productive process, labor activity moves "*to the side* of the production process instead of being its chief actor" (*Grundrisse*: 705). This placing of labor activity "to the side" of the immediate process of production indicates, Marx adds, that labor corresponds more and more to "a supervisory and regulatory activity" (ibid., 709). In other words: the tasks of a worker or of a clerk no longer involve the completion of a single particular assignment, but the changing and intensifying of social cooperation. Please allow me to digress. The concept of *social cooperation*, which is so complex and subtle in Marx, can be thought of in two different ways. There is, first of all, an "objective" meaning: each individual does different, specific, things which are put in relation to one another by the engineer or by the factory foreman: cooperation, in this case, transcends individual activity; it has no relevance to the way in which individual workers function. Secondly, however, we must consider also a "subjective" notion of cooperation: it materializes when a conspicuous portion of individual work consists of developing, refining, and intensifying cooperation itself. With post-Fordism the second definition of cooperation prevails. I am going to try to explain this better by means of a comparison. From the beginning, one resource of capitalistic enterprise has been the so-called "misappropriation of workers' know how." That is to say: when workers found a way to execute their labor with less effort, taking an extra break, etc., the corporate hierarchy took advantage of this minimal victory, knowing it was happening, in order to modify the organization of labor. In my opinion, a significant change takes place when the task of the worker or of the clerk to some extent consists in actually finding, in discovering expedients, "tricks," solutions which ameliorate the organization of labor. In the latter case, workers' knowledge is not used on the sly but it is requested explicitly; that is to say, it becomes one of the stipulated working assignments. The same change takes place, in fact, with regards to cooperation: it is not the same thing if workers are coordinated de facto by the engineer or if they are asked to invent and produce new cooperative procedures. Instead of remaining in the background, the act of cooperating, linguistic integration, comes to the very foreground.

When "subjective" cooperation becomes the primary productive force, labor activities display a marked linguistic-communicative quality, they entail the presence of others. The monological feature of labor dies away: the relationship with others is a driving, basic element, not something accessory. Where labor moves *to the side* of the immediate productive process, instead of being one of its components, productive cooperation is a "publicly organized space." This "publicly organized space"—interjected into the labor process—mobilizes attitudes which are traditionally political. Politics (in the broad sense) becomes productive force, task, "tool box." One could say that the heraldic motto of post-Fordism is, rightfully, "politics above all." After all, what else could the discourse of "total quality" mean, if not a request to surrender to production a taste for action, the capacity to face the possible and the unforeseen, the capacity to communicate something new?

When hired labor involves the desire for action, for a relational capacity, for the presence of others—all things that the preceding generation was trying out within the local party headquarters—we can say that some distinguishing traits of the human animal, above all the possession of a language, are subsumed within capitalistic production. The inclusion of the very *anthropogenesis* in the existing mode of production is an extreme event. Forget the Heideggerian chatter about the "technical era"... This event does not assuage, but radicalizes, instead, the antinomies of economic-social capitalistic formation. Nobody is as poor as those who see their own relation to the presence of others, that is to say, their own communicative faculty, their own possession of a language, reduced to wage labor.

Intellect as score

If the entirety of post-Fordist labor is productive (of surplus-value) labor precisely because it functions in a political-virtuosic manner, then the question to ask is this: what is the *score* which the virtuosos-workers perform? What is the script of their linguistic-communicative *performances*?

The pianist performs a Chopin waltz, the actor is more or less faithful to a preliminary script, the orator has at the least some notes to refer to; all performing artists can count on a score. But when virtuosity applies to the totality of social labor, which one is the proper score? From my perspective, I maintain without too many reservations that the score performed by the multitude in the post-Ford era is the Intellect, intellect as generic human faculty. According to Marx, the score of modern virtuosos is the *general intellect*, the general intellect of society, abstract thought which has become a pillar of social production. We thus go back to a theme (*general intellect*, public intellect, "commonplaces," etc.) which we considered during the first day.

By *general intellect* Marx means science, knowledge in general, the know-how on which social productivity relies by now. The politicization of work (that is, the subsumption into the sphere of labor of what had hitherto belonged to political action) occurs precisely when thought becomes the primary source of the production of wealth. Thought ceases to be an invisible activity and becomes something exterior, "public," as it breaks into the productive process. One could say: only then, only when it has linguistic intellect as its barycenter, can the activity of labor absorb into itself many of the characteristics which had previously belonged to the sphere of political action.

Up to this point we have discussed the juxtaposition between Labor and Politics. Now, however, the third facet of human experience comes into play, Intellect. It is the "score" which is always performed, over and again, by the workers-virtuosos. I believe that the hybridization between the different spheres (pure thought, political life and labor) begins precisely when the Intellect, as principal productive force, becomes public. Only then does labor assume a virtuosic (or communicative) semblance, and, thus, it colors itself with "political" hues.

Marx attributes to thought an exterior character, a public disposition, on two different occasions. Above all, when he makes use of the expression "real abstraction," which is a very beautiful expression also from a philosophical point of view, and then, when he discusses "*general intellect.*" Money, for instance, is a real abstraction. Money, in fact, embodies, makes *real,* one of the cardinal principles of human thought: the idea of equivalency. This idea, which is in itself utterly abstract, acquires a concrete existence, even jingles inside a wallet. A thought becoming a *thing*: here is what a real abstraction is. On the other hand, the concept of *general intellect* does nothing but advance, excessively, the notion of real abstraction. With the term *general intellect* Marx indicates the stage in which certain realities (for instance, a coin) no longer have the value and validity of a thought, but rather it is our thoughts, as such, that immediately acquire the value of material facts. If in the case of abstract thought it is the empirical fact (for example, the exchange of equivalencies) which exhibits the sophisticated structure of pure thought, in the case of *general intellect* the relation is overturned: now it is our thoughts which present themselves with the weight and incidence typical of facts. The *general intellect* is the stage at which mental abstractions are immediately, in themselves, real abstractions.

Here, however, is where the problems arise. Or, if you wish, a certain dissatisfaction arises with relation to Marx's formulations. The difficulty derives from the fact that Marx conceives the "general intellect" as a scientific objectified capacity, as a system of machines. Obviously, this aspect of the "general intellect" matters, but it is not everything. We should consider the dimension where the general intellect, instead of being incarnated (or rather, *cast in iron*) into the system of machines, exists as attribute of living labor. The *general intellect* manifests itself today, above all, as the communication, abstraction, self-reflection of living subjects. It seems legitimate to maintain that, according to the very logic of economic development, it is necessary that a part of the *general intellect* not congeal as fixed capital but unfold in communicative interaction, under the guise of epistemic paradigms, dialogical *performances*, linguistic games. In other words, public intellect is one and the same as cooperation, the acting in concert of human labor, the communicative competence of individuals.

In the fifth chapter of the first book of the *Capital*, Marx writes: "The labour process, as we have just presented it in its simple and abstract elements, is purposeful activity aimed at the production of use-values [...] We did not, therefore, have to present the worker in his relationship with other workers; it was enough to present man and his labour on one side, nature and its materials on the other"(*Capital*, Volume 1: 290). In this chapter Marx describes the labor process as a natural process of organic renewal between humans and nature, thus in abstract and general terms, without paying attention to historical-social relations. Nonetheless, we should ask whether it is legitimate, while remaining on this very general (almost anthropological) level, to expurgate from the concept of labor the interactive aspect, one's relation with other workers. It is certainly not legitimate as long as the activity of labor has its core in communicative performance. It is impossible, then, to trace the process of labor without presenting, from the beginning, the worker in relation with other workers; or, if we wish to employ again the category of virtuosity, in relation with one's "public."

The concept of cooperation comprises in itself, fully, the communicative capacity of human beings. That is true, above all, where cooperation is truly a specific "product" of the activity of labor, something which is promoted, elaborated, refined by those who cooperate. The *general intellect* demands virtuosic action (that is, in the broad sense, political action), precisely because a consistent portion of this intellect is not channeled in the machine system, but manifests itself in the direct activity of human labor, in its linguistic cooperation.

The intellect, the pure faculty of thought, the simple fact of having-a-language: let us repeat, here lies the "score" which is always and again performed by the post-Fordist virtuosos. (We should notice the difference in approach between today's lecture and that of our previous seminar: what today we are calling the "score" of the virtuoso, the intellect, in our previous meeting was seen as an apotropaic resource, as shelter against the indeterminate hazards of the worldly context. It is important to consider both of these concepts together: the contemporary multitude, with its forms of life and its linguistic games, places itself at the crossroads between these two meanings of "public intellect.") I would like to go back to, and emphasize here, an important point I have made before. While the virtuoso in the strictest sense of the word (the pianist, the dancer, for instance) makes use of a well defined score, that is to say, of an *end product* in its most proper and restricted sense, the post-Fordist virtuosos, "performing" their own linguistic faculties, can not take for granted a determined *end product*. *General intellect* should not necessarily mean the aggregate of the knowledge acquired by the species, but the *faculty* of thinking; potential as such, not its countless particular realizations. The "general intellect" is nothing but the *intellect in general*. Here it is useful to go back to the example of the speaker which we have already examined. With the infinite potential of one's own linguistic faculty as the only "score," a locutor (any locutor) articulates determined acts of speech: so then, the faculty of language is the opposite of a determined script, of an end product with these or those unmistakable characteristics. Virtuosity for the post-Fordist multitude is one and the same as the virtuosity of the speaker: virtuosity without a script, or rather, based on the premise of a script that coincides with pure and simple *dynamis*, with pure and simple potential.

It is useful to add that the relation between "score" and virtuosic performance is regulated by the norms of capitalistic enterprise. Putting to work (and to profit) the most generic communicative and cognitive faculties of the human animal has a historical index, a historically determined form. The *general intellect* manifests itself, today, as a perpetuation of wage labor, as a hierarchical system, as a pillar of the production of surplus-value.

Reason of State and Exit

At this point we can sketch some of the consequences of the hybridization between Labor, (political) Action and Intellect. Consequences which occur both on the level of production and within the public sphere (State, administrative apparatus).

The Intellect becomes public as soon as it links itself to labor; we must observe, however, that once it has been linked to wage labor, its typical publicness is also inhibited and distorted. This publicness is evoked over and over again in its role as productive force; and it is suppressed over and over again in its role as *public sphere* (in the proper sense of the term), as possible root of political Action, as a different constitutional principle.

The *general intellect* is the foundation of a social cooperation broader than that cooperation which is specifically related to labor. Broader and, at the same time, totally heterogeneous. We go back to one of the themes addressed during the first day of our seminar. While the connections of the productive process are based on a technical and hierarchical *division* of tasks, the acting in concert which hinges upon the *general intellect* moves from common participation to "life of the mind," that is, from the preliminary *sharing* of communicative and cognitive abilities. However, cooperation *in excess* of the Intellect, instead of annulling the co-actions of capitalistic production, figures as its most eminent resource. Its heterogeneity has neither voice nor visibility. On the contrary, since the appearance of the Intellect becomes the technical prerequisite of Labor, the acting in concert beyond labor which it brings about is in turn subsumed into the criteria and hierarchies which characterize the regime of the factory.

There are two principal consequences of this paradoxical situation. The first pertains to the nature and form of political power. The peculiar publicness of the Intellect, deprived of its own true expression by that very Labor which at the same time reclaims it as productive power, manifests itself indirectly within the sphere of the State by way of a *hypertrophic growth of the administrative apparatus*. The administration, and no longer the political-parliamentary system, is the heart of "stateness" ["statualità"]: but this is so, in fact, because the administration represents an authoritarian coalescence of the *general intellect*, the point of fusion between knowledge and control, the inverted image of excess cooperation. It is true that people have noticed for years the increasing and determining weight of bureaucracy within the "body politic," the preeminence of the decree with respect to the law: here, however, I would like to indicate a new threshold. In short, we no longer face the well-known processes of rationalization of the State; on the contrary, we must acknowledge the achieved *statization* [*statizzazione*] *of the Intellect* which has occurred. The old expression "reason of State" acquires for the first time a non-metaphorical significance. Hobbes saw the principle of legitimization of absolute power in the *transfer* of the natural right of each single individual to the person of the sovereign; now, on the other hand, we should talk about a *transfer* of the Intellect, or rather, of its immediate and irreducible publicness to the state administration.

The second consequence pertains to the prevailing nature of the post-Fordist regime. Since the "publicly organized space" opened up by the Intellect is constantly reduced to labor cooperation, that is, to a thick net of hierarchical relations, the nullifying function of the "presence of others" in all concrete operations of production takes the form of *personal dependence*. In other words, virtuosic activity shows itself as universal *servile work*. The affinity between a pianist and a waiter, which Marx had foreseen, finds an unexpected confirmation in the epoch in which all wage labor has something in common with the "performing artist." It is just that the very labor which produces the surplus-value is what takes on the appearance of servile labor. When "the product is inseparable from the act of producing," this act calls into question the personhood of the one who performs the work and, above all, the relation of this personhood to that of the one who has commissioned the work or for whom it is being done. Putting to work that which is *common*, that is, the intellect and language, renders the impersonal technical division of tasks fictitious, because such community does not translate into a public sphere (that is to say, into a political community); but is also induces a viscous personalization of subjection.

The crucial question goes like this: is it possible to split that which today is united, that is, the Intellect (the *general intellect*) and (wage) Labor, and to unite that which today is divided, that is, Intellect and political Action? Is it possible to move from the "ancient alliance" of Intellect/Labor to a "new alliance" of Intellect/political Action?

Rescuing political action from its current paralysis is no different from developing the publicness of the Intellect outside the realm of wage Labor, in opposition to it. This matter shows two distinct profiles, between which, however, there exists the strongest complementary bond. On one hand, the *general intellect* asserts itself as an autonomous public sphere only if the juncture that ties it to the production of goods and wage labor is severed. On the other hand, the subversion of capitalistic relations of production can manifest itself, at this point, only with the institution of a *non-state run public sphere*, of a political community that hinges on the *general intellect*. The salient traits of post-Fordist experience (servile virtuosity, exploitation of the very faculty of language, unfailing relation to the "presence of others," etc.) postulate, as a form of conflictual retaliation, nothing less than a radically new form of democracy.

The *non-state run public sphere* is a public sphere which conforms to the way of being of the multitude. It benefits from the "publicness" of language/thought, of the extrinsic, conspicuous, shared character of the Intellect in the guise of a score for the virtuosos. It is a "publicness"—as we have already observed during the first day of our seminar—totally heterogeneous with respect to that which is instituted by state sovereignty, or to quote Hobbes, "by the unity of the body politic." This "publicness," which manifests itself today as an eminent productive resource, can become a constitutional principle, a *public sphere*, in fact.

How is non-servile virtuosity possible? How do we move, hypothetically, from a servile virtuosity to a "republican" virtuosity (understanding "republic of the multitude" to mean a sphere of common affairs which is no longer state-run)? How do we conceive, in principle, of political action based on the *general intellect*? We must tread this terrain carefully. All we can do is to point to the *logical form* of something that is still lacking a solid empirical experience. I am proposing two key-terms: civil disobedience and exit.

"Civil disobedience" represents, perhaps, the fundamental form of political action of the multitude, provided that the multitude is emancipated from the liberal tradition within which it is encapsulated. It is not a matter of ignoring a specific law because it appears incoherent or contradictory to other fundamental norms, for example to the constitutional charter. In such case, in fact, reluctance would signal only a deeper loyalty to state control. Conversely, the radical disobedience which concerns us here casts doubt on the State's actual ability to control. Let us digress for a moment in order to understand this better.

According to Hobbes, with the institution of the "body politic," we force ourselves to obey *before* we even know what we will be ordered to do: "our obligation to civil obedience, by vertue whereof the civill Lawes are valid, is before all civill Lawe" (*De Cive*, Chap. XIV, Section XXI). For this reason we shall not find a particular law which explicitly dictates that people should not revolt. If the unconditional acceptance of the controlling power were not already *presupposed*, the concrete legislative presuppositions (including, obviously, that which states "thou shalt not rebell") would have no validity whatsoever. Hobbes maintains that the initial bond of obedience derives from "Lawes of nature," that is from a common interest in self-preservation and security. Still, he quickly adds that this "natural law," the Super-law which compels people to observe all of the orders of the sovereign, effectively becomes law only when we have left the state of nature, thus when the State has already been instituted. Thus, a real paradox takes shape: the duty to obey is both the cause and the effect of the existence of the State; this duty is supported by the very State which depends upon it for the constitution of its own foundation; it precedes *and* follows, at the same time, the development of a "supreme empire."

So then, the multitude aims precisely at this preliminary form of obedience without content, which is the foundation solely of the gloomy dialectic between acquiescence and "transgression." By breaking a particular law meant for dismantling socialized medicine or for stopping immigration, the multitude goes back to the covert presupposition hidden behind every act of mandating law and taints its ability to remain in force. Radical disobedience also "precedes civil laws," since it is not limited to the breaking of these laws but also calls into question the very foundation of their validity.

And now let us move on to the second key word: exit. The breeding ground of disobedience does not lie exclusively in the social conflicts which express *protest*, but, and above all, in those which express *defection* (as Albert O. Hirschman has explained [Hirschman, *Exit*]: not as *voice* but as *exit*).

Nothing is less passive than the act of fleeing, of exiting. Defection modifies the conditions within which the struggle takes place, rather than presupposing those conditions to be an unalterable horizon; it modifies the context within which a problem has arisen, rather than facing this problem by opting for one or the other of the provided alternatives. In short, *exit* consists of unrestrained invention which alters the rules of the game and throws the adversary completely off balance. While remembering what was discussed on this subject during the first day of our seminar, we need only think of the mass exodus from the regime of the factory, carried out by American workers in the middle of the nineteenth century. By venturing into the "frontier" to colonize inexpensive land, they seized upon the opportunity to reverse their own initial condition. Something similar took place in the late Seventies in Italy, when the young labor-power, challenging all expectations, chose temporary and part-time work over full-time employment in big corporations. Though it lasted only for a brief period, professional mobility functioned as a political resource, giving rise to the eclipse of industrial discipline and allowing for the establishing of a certain degree of self-determination.

Exit, or defection, is the polar opposite of the desperate cry "there is nothing to lose but one's own chains:" on the contrary, exit hinges on a latent kind of wealth, on an exuberance of possibilities, in short, on the principle of the *tertium datur*. But for the contemporary multitude, what is this virtual abundance which presses for the flee-option at the expense of the resistance-option? What is at stake, obviously, is not a spatial "frontier," but the surplus of knowledge, communication, virtuosic acting in concert, all presupposed by the publicness of the *general intellect*. Defection allows for a dramatic, autonomous, and affirmative expression of this surplus; and in this way it impedes the "transfer" of this surplus into the power of state administration, impedes its configuration as productive resource of the capitalistic enterprise.

Disobedience, exit. It is clear, however, that these are only allusions to what the true *political*, and not servile, virtuosity of the multitude could be.

Multitude as Subjectivity

Day Three

The concept of multitude merits perhaps the same treatment which the great French epistemologist Gaston Bachelard proposed using for the problems and paradoxes brought about by quantum mechanics. Bachelard maintained (Bachelard, *The Philosophy of No*) that quantum mechanics must be understood as a grammatical subject and that in order for it to be adequately thought out, one must make use of many philosophical "predicates" which are *heterogeneous*: sometimes a Kantian concept is useful, at other times a notion inspired by *Gestalt* psychology, or even some subtle idea of scholastic logic. This is also true in our case. The multitude must also be investigated by means of concepts derived from different areas of study and different authors.

This is what we began to do during the course of the initial two days of our seminar. During the first day we approached the subject of the mode of being of the "many" by way of the dialectic dread-refuge. As you will recall, we employed key words from Hobbes, Kant, Heidegger, Aristotle (*topoi koinoi*, the "common places"), Marx and Freud. During the second day, instead, we continued the investigation of the contemporary multitude by discussing the juxtaposition between poiesis and praxis, Labor and political Action. The "predicates" we utilized in this regard were drawn from Hannah Arendt, Glenn Gould, the novelist Luciano Bianciardi, Saussure, Guy Debord, and once again Marx, Hirshmann and others. Today we will examine another group of concepts which will enable us, I hope, to shed light, from a different perspective, on the multitude. The new angle of perspective will come from the *forms of subjectivity*.

The predicates we will attribute to the grammatical subject of "multitude" are: a) the principle of individuation, that is, the ancient philosophical question which hinges on what enables singularity to be singular and an individual to be individual; b) Foucault's notion of "bio-politics"; c) emotional tonalities, or *Stimmungen*, which define, today, the forms of life of the "many:" opportunism and cynicism (let us note, however: by emotional tonality I do not mean a passing psychological rippling, but a characteristic relation with one's own being in the world); d) lastly, two phenomena, which, analyzed also by Augustine and by Pascal, rise to the rank of philosophical themes in Heidegger's *Being and Time*: idle talk and curiosity.

The principle of individuation

Multitude signifies: plurality—literally: being-many—as a lasting form of social and political existence, as opposed to the cohesive unity of the people. Thus, multitude consists of a network of *individuals*; the many are a *singularity*.

The crucial point is to consider these singularities as a point of arrival, not as a starting point; as the ultimate result of a *process of individuation*, not as solipsistic atoms. Precisely because they are the complex result of a progressive differentiation, the "many" do not postulate an ulterior synthesis. The individual of the multitude is the final stage of a process beyond which there is nothing else, because everything else (the passage from the One to the Many) has already taken place.

When we speak of a process, or a principle, of individuation, we should keep clearly in mind what precedes individuation itself. This has to do, first of all, with a *pre-individual reality*, that is to say, something common, universal and undifferentiated. The process which produces singularity has a non-individual, pre-individual *incipit*. Singularity takes its roots in its opposite, comes out of something that lies at its antipodes. The notion of multitude seems to share something with liberal thought because it values individuality but, at the same time, it distances itself from it radically because this individuality is the final product of a process of individuation which stems from the universal, the generic, the pre-individual. The seeming nearness is overturned and becomes the maximum distance.

Let us ask this question: what are the components of the pre-individual reality which is at the foundation of individuation? The possible answers are many and are all legitimate.

First of all, the pre-individual is the biological basis of the species, that is, the sensory organs, motor skills apparatus, perception abilities. In this regard, Merleau-Ponty maintains something very interesting (*Phenomenology*: 215): "I am no more aware of being the true subject of my sensation than of my birth or my death." And later in his study he writes: "sight, hearing and touch, with their fields, [...] are anterior, and remain alien, to my personal life" (ibid., 347). Perception cannot be encapsulated by the first person singular pronoun. It is never an individual "I" who hears, sees, touches; it is the whole species as such. To speak about the senses, the anonymous pronoun "one" seems more appropriate: *one* sees, *one* touches, *one* hears. The pre-individual nature inscribed in the senses is a generic biological endowment, which is not susceptible to individuation.

Secondly, language is pre-individual; it is the historical-natural language shared by all speakers of a certain community. Language belongs to everybody and to nobody. Also in the case of language, there is not an individual "I" but a "one": *one* speaks. The use of the spoken word is, at first, something *inter-psychic*, social, public. A "private language" does not exist—in any individual case, and even less in the case of an infant. In this respect one comprehends the full extent of the concept of "public intellect" or *general intellect*. Language, however, unlike sensory perception, is a pre-individual sphere within which is rooted the process of individuation. The ontogenesis, that is, the developmental phases of the individual human being, consists in fact of the passage from language as public or inter-psychic experience to language as singularizing and intra-psychic experience. This process, in my opinion, takes place when the child understands that the act of *parole* does not exclusively depend on the determined *langue* (which in many respects resembles an amniotic fluid or an anonymous zoological environment); rather, it stands in relation also to a generic *faculty* for speaking, to an indeterminate *capacity* for saying things (which is never resolved in one historical-natural language or another). The progressive clarification of the relation between the *faculty* (or capacity) for speaking and the particular act of *parole*: this is what enables us to surpass the pre-individual character of historical-natural language, pressing for the individuation of the speaker. In fact, while language belongs to everybody and to nobody, the passage from the pure and simple ability to say something to a particular and contingent utterance determines the space of an individual's notion of "my own." But this is a complicated matter and I have time here only to allude to it. In conclusion: we should keep in mind that, while the pre-individual perceptive faculty remains such, without giving way to an act of individuation, the pre-individual linguistic faculty is, on the other hand, the basis for individuated singularity, or the realm within which this singularity takes its form.

Thirdly, the prevailing relation of production is pre-individual. Thus, we face also a pre-individual reality which is essentially *historical*. In advanced capitalism, the labor process mobilizes the most universal requisites of the species: perception, language memory, and feelings. Roles and tasks, in the post-Ford era, correspond by and large to the *Gattungsgwesen* or "generic existence," which Marx discussed in *The Economic and Philosophic Manuscripts of*

1844. The entire realm of productive forces is pre-individual. It is social cooperation in the form of action in concert, the totality of poietic, "political," cognitive, emotional forces. It is the *general intellect*, the general, objective, external intellect. The contemporary multitude is composed of individualized individuals, who have behind them also *this* pre-individual reality (in addition, naturally, to anonymous sensory perception and to the language of everybody and nobody).

An amphibian Subject. An important text by Gilbert Simondon, a French philosopher and dear friend of Gilles Deleuze, is about to be published in Italy (by the publisher DeriveApprodi); this is a text which has hitherto been rather ignored (even in France, mind you). The book is entitled *L' individuation psychique et collective* (Simondon). Simondon's reflection on the principle of individuation presents other conceptual "predicates" to apply to the grammatical subject at hand, the multitude.

Two of Simondon's theses are particularly fitting to any discussion of subjectivity in the era of the multitude. The first thesis states that *individuation is never concluded*, that the pre-individual is never fully translated into singularity. Consequently, according to Simondon, the *subject* consists of the permanent interweaving of pre-individual elements and individuated characteristics; moreover, the subject *is* this interweaving. It would be a serious mistake, according to Simondon, to identify the subject with one of its components, the one which is singularized. The subject is, rather, a composite: "I," but also "one," unrepeatable uniqueness, but also anonymous universality.

While the individuated "I" cohabits with the biological basis of the species (sensory perception, etc.), with the public or inter-psychic characteristics of the mother tongue, with productive cooperation and the *general intellect*, we must add that this cohabitation is not always a peaceful one. Quite to the contrary, it engenders crises of various kinds. The subject is a battlefield. Not infrequently do pre-individual characteristics seem to call into question the act of individuation: the latter reveals itself to be a precarious, always reversible, result. At other times, on the other hand, it is the precise and exact "I" which appears to endeavor to reduce for itself, with feverish voracity, all of the pre-individual aspects of our experience. In both cases, there is no shortage of the manifestation of dread-panic, angst, pathologies of various kinds. Either an "I" that no longer has a world or a world that no longer has an "I": these are the two extremes of an oscillation which, though appearing in more contained forms, is never totally absent. This oscillation is prominently signaled, according to Simondon, by feelings and passions. The relation between pre-individual and individuated is, in fact, mediated by feelings.

Incidentally, the not always harmonious interweaving of pre-individual and singularized aspects of the subject, upon close examination, concerns the relation between each one of the "many" and the *general intellect*. On the first day of our seminar we emphasized as much as necessary the harrowing physiognomy that can be assumed by the "general intellect" in the event that the general intellect is not translated into a public sphere and ends up, instead, oppressing in the form of an impersonal and despotic power. In such case, the pre-individual becomes menacing and overwhelming. Twentieth century critical thought—above all, the Frankfurt School—maintained that unhappiness derives from the separation of the individual from the universal productive forces. We imagine an individual confined to a cold and damp niche, while, far away from this individual, there gleams forth the anonymous power of society (and of the species). This is a totally erroneous idea. Unhappiness and insecurity do not derive from the separation between individual existence and pre-individual powers, but from their absolute interweaving, when this interweaving manifests itself as disharmony, pathological oscillation, and crisis.

Let us now turn to the second of Simondon's theses. It states that the collective, the collective experience, the life of the group, is not, as we usually believe, the sphere within which the salient traits of a singular individual diminish or disappear; on the contrary, it is the terrain of a new and more radical individuation. By participating in a collective, the subject, far from surrendering the most unique individual traits, has the opportunity to individuate, at least in part, the share of pre-individual reality which all individuals carry within themselves. According to Simondon, within the collective we endeavor to refine our singularity, to bring it to its climax. Only within the collective, certainly not within the isolated subject, can perception, language, and productive forces take on the shape of an individuated experience.

This thesis allows us to have a better understanding of the opposition between "people" and "multitude." For the multitude, the collective is not centripetal or coalescent. It is not the locus in which the "general will" is formed and state unity is prefigured. Since the collective experience of the multitude radicalizes, rather than dulling, the process of individuation, the idea that from such experience one could extrapolate a homogeneous trait is to be excluded as a matter of principle; it is also to be excluded that one could "delegate" or "transfer" something to the sovereign. The *collective of the multitude*, seen as ulterior or second degree individuation, establishes the feasibility of a *non-representational democracy*. Conversely, we can define a "non-representational democracy" as an individuation of the historical-social pre-individual: science, knowledge, productive cooperation, *and general intellect*. The "many" persevere as "many" without aspiring to the unity of the state because: 1) as individuated singularities they have already left behind the unity/universality intrinsic to the diverse species of the pre-individual; 2) through their collective action they underscore and further the process of individuation.

The social individual. In the "Fragment on Machines" (*Grundrisse*: 705) Marx coins a concept which, in my view, is central to comprehending the subjectivity of the contemporary multitude. This is a concept, let me say immediately, which is objectively related to Simondon's thesis on the interweaving of pre-individual reality and singularity. It is the concept of the "social individual." It is not by accident, it seems to me, that Marx utilizes this expression in the same pages where he discusses the *general intellect*, the public intellect. The individual is *social* because within the individual the *general intellect* is present. Or also, to return to Marx in his *Economic and Philosophic Manuscripts of 1844*, the individual is social because the individual is an open manifestation, standing alongside the singular "I," the *Gattungswesen*, "generic existence," the totality of requisites and faculties of the *Homo sapiens* species.

The term "social individual" is an oxymoron, a unity of opposites: it could appear to be some sort of Hegelian whimsy, suggestive and insubstantial, were we not able to benefit from Simondon in deciphering its sense. "Social" should be translated as pre-individual, and "individual" should be seen as the ultimate result of the process of *individuation*. Since the term "pre-individual" must include sensory perception, language, and productive forces, we could also say that the "social individual" is the individual who openly exhibits a unique ontogenesis, a unique development (with its own different layers or constituent elements).

There is a sort of lexical chain that ties together the being-many, the ancient question of the principle of individuation, the Marxian notion of "social individual," Simondon's thesis on the cohabitation within each subject of pre-individual elements (language, social cooperation, etc.) and individuated elements. I propose calling the combination of "social individuals" the multitude. We could say—with Marx, but against the grain of a large segment of Marxism—that the radical transformation of the present state of things consists in bestowing maximum prominence and maximum value on the existence of every single member of the species. It may seem paradoxical, but I believe that Marx's theory could (or rather should) be understood, today, as a realistic and complex theory of the individual, as a rigorous individualism: thus, as a theory of individuation.

An equivocal concept: bio-politics

Foucault introduced the term "bio-politics" in some courses he taught in the Seventies at the Collège de France (see Foucault). The term was applied to the changes which took place in the concept of "population" between the end of the eighteenth and the beginning of the nineteenth century. In Foucault's view, it is during this period that life, life as such, life as mere biological process, begins to be governed and administered politically. The concept of "bio-politics" has recently become fashionable: it is often, and enthusiastically, invoked in every kind of context. We should avoid this automatic and unreflective use of the term. Let us ask ourselves, then, how and why life breaks through to the center of the public scene, how and why the State regulates and governs it.

In my opinion, to comprehend the rational core of the term "bio-politics," we should begin with a different concept, a much more complicated concept from a philosophical standpoint: that of *labor-power*. This is a concept discussed everywhere in the social sciences, where its harsh and paradoxical character is however, carelessly avoided. If professional philosophers were to get involved in something serious here, they would have to devote much effort and attention to it. What does "labor-power" mean? It means *potential* to produce. Potential, that is to say, aptitude, capacity, *dynamis*. Generic, undetermined potential: where one particular type of labor or another has not been designated, but *any* kind of labor is taking place, be it the manufacturing of a car door, or the harvesting of pears, the babble of someone calling in to a phone "party-line," or the work of a proofreader. Labor-power is "the aggregate of those mental and physical capabilities existing in the physical form, the living personality, of a human being" (*Capital*, Volume 1: 270). *All of those capabilities*, we should note well. By talking about labor-power we implicitly refer to every sort of faculty: linguistic competence, memory, motility, etc. Only in today's world, in the post-Ford era, is the reality of labor-power fully up to the task of realizing itself. Only in today's world, that is to say, can the notion of labor-power not be reduced (as it was at the time of Gramsci) to an aggregate of physical and mechanical attributes; now, instead, it encompasses within itself, and rightfully so, the "life of the mind."

But let us get to the point here. The capitalistic production relation is based on the difference between labor-power and effective labor. Labor-power, I repeat, is pure *potential*, quite distinct from its correspondent acts. Marx writes: "When we speak of capacity for labour, we do not speak of labour, any more than we speak of digestion when we speak of capacity for digestion" (*Capital*, Volume 1: 277). We are dealing here, however, with a potential which boasts of the extremely concrete prerogatives of commodities. Potential is something non-present, non-real; but in the case of labor-power, this non-present something is subject to the laws of supply and demand (Virno, *Il ricordo*: 121-3). Capitalists buy the *capacity* for producing as such ("the sum of all physical and intellectual aptitudes which exist in the material world"), and not simply one or more specific services. After the sale has occurred, capitalists can use as they please the commodity which has been acquired. "The purchaser of labour-power consumes it by setting the seller of it to work. By working, the latter becomes in actuality what previously he only was potentially "(*Capital*, Volume 1: 283). Labor which has actually been paid out does not simply reimburse the capitalist for the money spent previously in order to assure the other's potential for working; it continues for an additional period of time. Here lies the genesis of surplus-value, here lies the mystery of capitalistic accumulation.

Labor-power incarnates (literally) a fundamental category of philosophical thought: specifically, the potential, the *dynamis*. And "potential," as I have just said, signifies that which is *not* current, that which is *not* present. Well then, something which is not present (or real) becomes, with capitalism, an exceptionally important commodity. This potential, *dynamis*, non-presence, instead of remaining an abstract concept, takes on a pragmatic, empirical, socioeconomic dimension. The potential as such, when it still has not been applied, is at the core of the exchange between capitalist and worker. The object of the sale is not a real entity (labor services actually executed) but something which, in and of itself, does not have an autonomous spacial-temporal existence (the generic ability to work).

The paradoxical characteristics of labor-power (something unreal which is, however, bought and sold as any other commodity) are the premise of biopolitics. In order to understand it, however, we must go through another step in the argument. In the *Grundrisse* Marx writes that "the use value which the worker has to offer to the capitalist, which he has to offer to others in general, is not materialized in a product, does not exist apart from him at all, thus exists not really, but only in *potentiality*, as his *capacity*" (*Grundrisse*: 267; Virno's italics). Here is the crucial point: where something which exists only as *possibility* is sold, this something is not separable from the *living person* of the seller. The living body of the worker is the substratum of that labor-power which, in itself, has no independent existence. "Life," pure and simple *bios*, acquires a specific importance in as much as it is the tabernacle of *dynamis*, of mere potential.

Capitalists are interested in the life of the worker, in the body of the worker, only for an indirect reason: this life, this body, are what contains the faculty, the potential, the *dynamis*. The living body becomes an object to be governed not for its intrinsic value, but because it is the substratum of what really matters: labor-power as the aggregate of the most diverse human faculties (the potential for speaking, for thinking, for remembering, for acting, etc.). Life lies at the center of politics when the prize to be won is immaterial (and in itself non-present) labor-power. For this reason, and this reason alone, it is legitimate to talk about "bio-politics." The living body which is a concern of the administrative apparatus of the State, is the tangible sign of a yet unrealized potential, the semblance of labor not yet objectified; as Marx says eloquently, of "labor as subjectivity." The potential for working, bought and sold just like another commodity, is labor not yet objectified, "labor as subjectivity." One could say that while money is the universal representation of the value of exchange—or rather of the exchangeability itself of products—life, instead, takes the place of the productive potential, of the invisible *dynamis*.

The non-mythological origin of that mechanism of expertise and power which Foucault defines as bio-politics can be traced back, without hesitation, to the mode of being of the labor-power. The practical importance taken on by potential as potential (the fact that it is bought and sold as such), as well as its inseparability from the immediate corporeal existence of the worker, is the real foundation of bio-politics. Foucault mocks libertarian theoreticians like Wilhelm Reich (the heterodox psychiatrist), who claims that a spasmodic attention to life is the result of a repressive intention: disciplining the body in order to raise the level of productivity of labor. Foucault is totally right, but he is taking aim at an easy target. It is true: the government of life is extremely varied and articulated, ranging from the confinement of impulses to the most unrestrained laxity, from punctilious prohibition to the showy display of tolerance, from the ghetto for the poor to extravagant Keynesian incomes, from the high-security prison to the Welfare State. Having said this, we still have to address a crucial question: why is life, as such, managed and controlled? The answer is absolutely clear: because it acts as the substratum of a mere faculty, labor-power, which has taken on the consistency of a commodity. It is not a question, here, of the productivity of actual labor, but of the exchangeability of the potential to work. By the mere fact that it can be bought and sold, this potential calls into question the repository from which it is indistinguishable, that is, the living body. What is more, it sheds light on this repository as an object of innumerable and differentiated governmental strategies.

One should not believe, then, that bio-politics includes within itself, as its own distinct articulation, the management of labor-power. On the contrary: bio-politics is merely an effect, a reverberation, or, in fact, one articulation of that primary fact—both historical and philosophical—which consists of the commerce of potential as potential. Bio-politics exists wherever that which pertains to the potential dimension of human existence comes into the forefront, into immediate experience: not the spoken word, but the capacity for speaking as such; not the labor which has actually been completed, but the generic capability of producing. The potential dimension of existence becomes conspicuous only, and exclusively, under the guise of labor-power. In this potential we see the compendium of all the different faculties and potentials of the human animal. In fact, "labor-power" does not designate one specific faculty, but the *entirety* of human faculties in as much as they are involved in productive praxis. "Labor-power" is not a proper noun; it is a common noun.

The emotional tonalities of the multitude

Now I would like to speak briefly about the *emotional situation* in which the contemporary multitude finds itself. With the expression "emotional situation" I do not refer, let it be clear, to a cluster of psychological tendencies, but to ways of being and feeling so pervasive that they end up being common to the most diverse contexts of experience (work, leisure, feelings, politics, etc.). The emotional situation, over and above being ubiquitous, is always *ambivalent*. That is, it can manifest itself as a form of consent as often as it can as a form of conflict, as often with the characteristics of resignation as with those of critical unease. To put it another way: the emotional situation has a *neutral core* subject to diverse, and even contrary, elaborations.

This neutral core points toward a fundamental mode of being. Now, it is certain that the emotional situation of the multitude today manifests itself with "bad sentiments": opportunism, cynicism, social integration, inexhaustible recanting, cheerful resignation. Yet it is necessary to rise up from these "bad sentiments" to the neutral core, namely to the fundamental mode of being, which, in principle, could give rise even to developments very different from those prevailing today. What is difficult to understand is that the antidote, so to speak, can be tracked down only in what for the moment appears to be poison.

The emotional situation of the multitude in the post-Ford era is characterized by the *immediate connection* between production and ethicality, "structure" and "superstructure," the revolutionizing of the work process and sentiments, technologies and the emotional tonalities, material developments and culture. Let us pause for a moment to consider this connection. What are the principal requirements of dependent workers today? To be accustomed to mobility, to be able to keep up with the most sudden conversions, to be able to adapt to various enterprises, to be flexible in switching from one set of rules to another, to have an aptitude for a kind of linguistic interaction as banalized as it is unilateral, to be familiar with managing among a limited amount of possible alternatives. Now, these requirements are not the fruit of industrial discipline; rather, they are the result of a socialization that has its center of gravity *outside of the workplace.* The "professionalism" which is actually required and offered consists of the abilities one acquires during a prolonged sojourn in a pre-work, or precarious, stage. That is to say: in the period of waiting for a job, those generically social talents are developed, as is getting in the habit of not developing lasting habits, all of which, once work is found, will act as true and real "tools of the trade."

The post-Fordist undertaking puts to good use this practice of not having routines, this training in precariousness and variability. But the decisive fact is a kind of socialization (and by this term I mean the relationship with the world, with others, and with oneself) which essentially comes about outside of the workplace, socialization essentially *beyond work.* These are the urban shocks which Benjamin was talking about, the proliferation of linguistic games, the uninterrupted variation of rules and techniques, which constitute the arena in which we find the formation of abilities and qualifications which, only later on, will become "professional" abilities and qualifications. A closer look reveals that this outside-of–the-workplace socialization (which then combines with the "official duties" in job descriptions in the post-Ford era) consists of experiences and sentiments in which the great philosophers and sociologists of the last century, from Heidegger and Simmel on, have recognized the distinctive traits of nihilism. Nihilism is a praxis which no longer enjoys a solid foundation, one made up of support structures and protective practices upon which one can rely. During the twentieth century, nihilism seemed to be a collateral counterpoint to the processes of rationalization both of production and of the State. That is to say: on one side, labor, on the other, the precariousness and changeable nature of urban life. Now, however, nihilism (the practice of not having established practices, etc.) has entered into production, has become a professional qualification, and has been *put to work.* Only one who is experienced in the haphazard changing nature of the forms of urban life knows how to behave in the *just in time* factories [Author's English term].

It is almost useless to add that, in this way, the model used by a large part of the sociological and philosophical tradition to represent the processes of "modernization" goes to pieces. According to that model, innovation (technological, emotional, ethical) shakes up traditional societies in which repetitive customs prevailed. Philomen and Baucis, the serene farmers whom Goethe describes in *Faust*, would be uprooted by the modern entrepreneur. None of this, today. One can no longer speak of "modernization" where innovation intervenes with an increasingly contracted regularity upon a scene characterized by rootlessness, by contingency, by anonymity, etc. The crucial point is that the current productive commotion benefits from, and finds its most prized resource in, all those elements which the model of modernization lists, instead, among its consequences: the uncertainty of expectations, the unpredictability of assignments, fragile identities, ever changing values. The advanced technologies do not provoke a "displacement," such as to dissipate a pre-existing "familiarity"; rather, they reduce to a *professional profile* the experience of the most radical kind of displacement itself. Nihilism, once hidden in the shadow of technical-productive power, becomes a fundamental ingredient of that power, a quality highly prized by the marketplace of labor.

This is the background upon which, above all, two not exactly edifying emotional tonalities stand out: *opportunism* and *cynicism*. Let us try to sift through these "bad sentiments," recognizing in them a way of being, which, in and of itself need not necessarily express itself in unappealing forms.

Opportunism: The roots of opportunism lie in an outside-of-the-workplace socialization marked by unexpected turns, perceptible shocks, permanent innovation, chronic instability. Opportunists are those who confront a flow of ever-interchangeable possibilities, making themselves available to the greater number of these, yielding to the nearest one, and then quickly swerving from one to another. This is a structural, sober, non-moralistic definition of opportunism. It is a question of a sensitivity sharpened by the changeable *chances*, a familiarity with the kaleidoscope of opportunities, an intimate relationship with the possible, no matter how vast. In the post-Ford era mode of production, opportunism acquires a certain *technical* importance. It is the cognitive and behavioral reaction of the contemporary multitude to the fact that routine practices are no longer organized along uniform lines; instead, they present a high level of unpredictability. Now, it is precisely this ability to maneuver among abstract and interchangeable opportunities which constitutes *professional quality* in certain sectors of post-Fordist production, sectors where the labor process is not regulated by a single particular goal, but by a *class of* equivalent *possibilities* to be specified one at a time. The information machine, rather than being a means to a single end, is an introduction to successive and "opportunistic" elaborations. Opportunism gains in value as an indispensable resource whenever the concrete labor process is permeated by a diffuse "communicative action" and thus no longer identifies itself solely with mute "instrumental action." Or, to return to a theme touched upon during the second day of the seminar, whenever Labor includes in itself the salient traits of political Action. After all, what else is opportunism if not one of the talents of the politician?

Cynicism: Cynicism is also connected with the chronic instability of forms of life and linguistic games. This chronic instability places in full view, during labor time as well as during free time, the naked *rules* which artificially structure the boundaries of action. The emotional situation of the multitude is characterized, precisely, by the extreme proximity of the "many" to the *rules* which animate individual contexts. At the base of contemporary cynicism lies the fact that men and women first of all experience rules, far more often than "facts," and far earlier than they experience concrete events. But to experience rules directly means also to recognize their conventionality and groundlessness. Thus, one is no longer immersed in a predefined "game," participating therein with true allegiance. Instead, one catches a glimpse of oneself in individual "games" which are destitute of all seriousness and obviousness, having become nothing more than a place for immediate *self-affirmation*—a self-affirmation which is all the more brutal and arrogant, in short, cynical, the more it draws upon, without illusions but with perfect momentary allegiance, those same rules which characterize conventionality and mutability.

I believe there is a very strong relationship between the *general intellect* and contemporary cynicism. Or to put it better: I think that cynicism is *one* of the possible ways of reacting to the *general intellect* (not the only way, certainly; the theme of the ambivalence of the emotional situation returns here). Let us give a clearer explanation of this connection. The general intellect is social knowledge turned into the principal productive force; it is the complex of cognitive paradigms, artificial languages, and conceptual clusters which animate social communication and forms of life. The *general intellect* distinguishes itself from the "real abstractions" typical of modernity, which are all anchored to the *principle of equivalence*. "Real abstraction" is, above all, money, which represents the commensurability of labor, of products, of subjects. Thus, the *general intellect* has nothing to do with the principle of equivalence. The models of social knowledge are not units of measurement; instead, they constitute the premise for operative heterogeneous possibilities. Techno-scientific codes and paradigms present themselves as an "immediate productive force," as *constructive principles*. They do not equalize anything; instead, they act as premise to every type of action.

The fact that abstract knowledge, rather than the exchange of equivalents, provides order for social relations is reflected in the contemporary figure of the *cynic*. Why? Because the principle of equivalency constituted the base, even though a contradictory one, for egalitarian ideologies which supported the ideal of a reciprocal recognition without constraints, let alone the ideal of universal and transparent linguistic communication. Vice versa, the *general intellect*, as a clear introduction to social practice, does not offer any unit of measurement for comparison. Cynics recognize, in the particular context in which they operate, both the preeminent role played by certain *cognitive premises* as well as the simultaneous absence of real *equivalences*. As a precaution, they repress the aspiration for a dialogue on equal terms. From the outset they renounce any search for an inter-subjective foundation for their praxis, as well as any claim to a standard of judgement which shares the nature of a moral evaluation. The fall of the principle of *equivalency*, so intimately related to the exchange of commodities, can be seen in the behavior of the cynic, in the impatient abandonment of the appeal for *equality*. Cynics reach the point where they entrust their self-affirmation precisely to the multiplication (and fluidification) of hierarchies and inequalities which the unexpected centrality of production knowledge seems to entail.

Opportunism and cynicism: without a doubt, "bad sentiments." Nevertheless, we can hypothesize that every conflict or protest on the part of the multitude will take root in the same manner of being (the aforementioned "neutral core") which, for the moment, manifests itself in these rather repugnant forms. The neutral core of the contemporary emotional situation, susceptible to opposing manifestations, consists of a familiarity with the possible, in so far as it is possible, and of an extreme proximity to the conventional rules which give structure to the differing contexts of action. This familiarity and this proximity, from which opportunism and cynicism now derive, make up an indelible, distinctive sign of the multitude.

Idle talk and curiosity

To conclude, I would like to reflect upon two noted and infamous phenomena of everyday life upon which Martin Heidegger has conferred the rank of philosophical themes. First of all, *idle talk*, that is to say, a contagious and prolific discourse without any solid structure, indifferent to content, which it only touches on from time to time. Next, *curiosity*, which is the insatiable voracity for the new in so far as it is new. It seems to me that these are two more predicates inherent in the grammatical subject "multitude," provided that, as will be seen, one uses at times Heidegger's words against Heidegger himself. In discussing "idle talk" I would like to focus upon a further facet of the relationship multitude/verbal language; "curiosity," instead, has to do with certain epistemological virtues of the multitude (it goes without saying that what is in question here is only a spontaneous epistemology, one which has not been thought out).

Idle talk and curiosity were analyzed by Heidegger in *Being and Time* (Heidegger, Sections 35 and 36). These were singled out as typical manifestations of the "unauthentic life," which is characterized by a conformist leveling of all feeling and all understanding. In the "unauthentic life" the impersonal pronoun "one" dominates uncontested: *one* says, *one* does, *one* believes this or that. In the words of Simondon, it is the pre-individual who dominates the scene, inhibiting any individuation whatsoever. This "one" is anonymous and pervasive. It nurtures reassuring certainties; it diffuses opinions that are always already shared. It is the faceless subject of media communication. This "one" feeds us idle talk and unleashes a curiosity that cannot be restrained.

This anonymous "one," chatty and nosy, conceals the salient trait of human existence: being in the world. Take heed: to belong to the world does not mean contemplating it in a disinterested fashion. Rather, this belonging indicates a pragmatic involvement. The relation with my vital context does not consist, above all, of acts of comprehension and representation, but of an adaptive practice, in the search for protection, of a practical orientation, of a manipulative intervention upon surrounding objects. For Heidegger, the authentic life seems to find its adequate expression in *labor*. In the first place, the world is a world-workshop, a complex of productive means and goals, the theater of a general readiness for entering the world of labor. According to Heidegger, this fundamental connection with the world is distorted by idle talk and curiosity. One who chatters and abandons oneself to curiosity *does not* work, is diverted from carrying out a determined task, and has suspended every serious responsibility "for taking care of things." This "one," along with being anonymous, is also *idle*. The world-workshop is transformed into a world-spectacle.

Let us ask ourselves this question: is it then true that idle talk and curiosity remain confined to the realm of free time and relaxation, outside of labor? On the basis of what has been argued throughout this seminar, should it not be supposed, rather, that these attitudes have become the pivot of contemporary production in which the act of communication dominates, and in which the ability to manage amid continual innovations is most valued?

Let us begin with this idle talk which positions itself in the preeminent role of social communication, with its independence from every bond or presupposition, with its full *autonomy*. Autonomy from predefined goals, from limiting tasks, from the obligation of giving a faithful reproduction of the truth. With idle talk the denotative correspondence between things and words reaches a new low. Discourse no longer requires an external legitimization, based upon the events which it concerns. It constitutes in itself an *event* consisting of itself, which is justified solely by the fact that it happens. Heidegger writes: "In the language which is spoken when one expresses oneself, there lies an average intelligibility; [...] the discourse which is communicated can be understood to a considerable extent, even if the hearer does not bring himself into such a kind of Being towards what the discourse is about as to have a primordial understanding of it" (*Being and Time*: 212). And he continues: "idle talk is the possibility of understanding everything without previously making the thing one's own"(ibid., 213).

Idle talk damages the referential paradigm. The crisis of this paradigm lies at the origin of the *mass media*. Once they have been freed from the burden of corresponding point by point to the non-linguistic world, terms can multiply indefinitely, generating one from the other. Idle talk has no foundation. This lack of foundation explains the fleeting, and at times vacuous, character of daily interaction. Nevertheless, this same lack of foundation authorizes invention and the experimentation of new discourses at every moment. Communication, instead of reflecting and transmitting that which exists, itself produces the states of things, unedited experiences, new facts. I am tempted to say that idle talk resembles *background noise*: insignificant in and of itself (as opposed to noises linked to particular phenomena, such as a running motorbike or a drill), yet it offers a sketch from which significant variances, unusual modulations, sudden articulations can be derived.

It seems to me that idle talk makes up the primary subject of the *post-Fordist virtuosity* discussed in the second day of our seminar. Virtuosos, as you will recall, are those who produce something which is not distinguishable, nor even separable, from the act of production itself. Virtuosos are simple locuters par excellence. But, now I would add to this definition the non-referenced speakers; that is, the speakers who, while speaking, reflect neither one nor another state of affairs, but determine new states of affairs by means of their very own words: those who, according to Heidegger, *engage in idle talk*. This idle talk is *performative*: words determine facts, events, states of affairs (Austin, *How to Do Things with Words*). Or, if you wish, it is in idle talk that it is possible to recognize the fundamental nature of performance: not "I bet," or "I swear," or "I take this woman as my wife," but, above all, "I speak." In the assertion "I speak," I *do* something by *saying* these words; moreover, I declare what it is that I do while I do it.

Contrary to what Heidegger presumes, not only is idle talk not a poor experience and one to be deprecated, but it directly concerns labor, and social production. Thirty years ago, in many factories there were signs posted that commanded: "Silence, men at work!" Whoever was at work kept quiet. One began "chatting" only upon leaving the factory or the office. The principle breakthrough in post-Fordism is that it has placed language into the workplace. Today, in certain workshops, one could well put up signs mirroring those of the past, but declaring: "Men at work here. Talk!"

A certain number of standard utterances is not what is required of the worker; rather, an informal act of communication is required, one which is flexible, capable of confronting the most diverse possibilities (along with a good dose of *opportunism*, however). Using terms from the philosophy of language, I would say it is not the *parole* but the *langue* which is mobilized, the very faculty of language, not any of its specific applications. This faculty, which is the generic power of articulating every sort of utterance, takes on an empirical importance precisely in computer language. There, in fact, it is not so much "what is said," as much as the pure and simple "ability to say" that counts.

Let us move on to curiosity. This theme also has as its subject the anonymous "one," the uncontested protagonist of the "unauthentic life." And curiosity, for Heidegger, also takes place outside of the labor process. The "seeing," which in the process of labor is completed at the conclusion of a particular task, in free time becomes agitated, mobile, fickle. Heidegger writes: "Concern may come to rest in the sense of one's interrupting the performance and taking a rest, or it can do so by getting it finished. In rest, concern does not disappear; circumspection, however, becomes free and is no longer bound to the world of work" (ibid., 217). The liberation from the world of labor means that the "circumspection" feeds on any individual thing, fact, or event, all of which are reduced, however, to so many mere spectacles.

Heidegger cites Augustine, who drew a wonderful analysis, in the tenth book of the *Confessions*, from the notion of curiosity. The curious person, according to Augustine, is the person who indulges in the *concupiscentia oculorum*, in the greed of sight, longing to witness unusual and even horrible spectacles: "When the senses demand pleasure, they look for objects of visual beauty, harmonious sounds, fragrant perfumes, and things that are pleasant to the taste or soft to the touch. But when their motive is curiosity, they may look for just the reverse of these things [...] from a relish for investigation and discovery. What pleasure can there be in the sight of a mangled corpse, which can only horrify? Yet people will flock to see one lying on the ground, simply for the sensation of sorrow and horror that it gives them" (*Confessions*: Book X, Section 35). Both Augustine and Heidegger consider curiosity to be a degraded and perverse form of love for knowledge. In sum, a *deductive passion.* It is the plebeian parody of the *bios theoretikos*, of the contemplative life devoted to pure knowing. Neither the philosopher nor the curious person has practical interests;

both aim toward a learning experience for its own sake, toward a vision without extrinsic goals. But, with curiosity the senses usurp the prerogatives of thought: the eyes of the body, not the metaphorical eyes of the mind, are the ones which observe, search, evaluate all phenomena. The aesthetic *theoria* is transformed into the *voyeur's* "craving for experience, for knowledge."

Heidegger's judgement is definitive: in curiosity a radical estrangement lies hidden; the curious spirit "lets itself be carried along [mitnehmen] solely by the looks of the world; in this kind of Being, it concerns itself with becoming rid of itself as Being-in-the-world" (*Being and Time*: 216). I would like to compare Heidegger's judgement with Walter Benjamin's position. In "The Work of Art in the Age of Mechanical Reproduction" (Benjamin, *Illuminations*: 217–251) Benjamin proposes a diagnosis of the "one," of the ways of being of mass societies, in sum, of the "unauthentic life." Of course, he uses different terminology. And he arrives at conclusions that are very different with respect to Heidegger's. That which Heidegger considers to be a threat, Benjamin understands to be a promise, or at least an important opportunity. The technical reproduction of art and of every sort of experience, made possible through the mass media, is nothing other than the instrument which can most adequately satisfy a universal and omnivorous curiosity. But Benjamin praises that "craving for knowledge" by means of the senses, that "greed of sight" which Heidegger, instead, denigrates. Let us look at this in more detail.

Both curiosity (for Heidegger) and technical reproduction (for Benjamin) strive to *abolish distances*, to place everything within hand's reach (or better, within viewing distance). This inclination towards closeness assumes, however, an opposite meaning for the two authors. For Heidegger, in the absence of a laborious "taking care of things," the approaching of what is distant and estranged has the sole result of ruinously canceling perspective: the gaze can no longer distinguish between "foreground" and "background." When all things converge in an undifferentiated closeness (as happens, according to Heidegger, to those who are curious), there is less chance of having a stable center from which to observe these things. Curiosity resembles a flying carpet which, eluding the force of gravity, circles around at low altitude above phenomena (without taking root in them). With regard to mass-media curiosity, Benjamin, on the other hand, speaks of "the desire of contemporary masses to bring things 'closer' spatially and humanly, which is just as ardent as their bent toward overcoming the uniqueness of every reality by accepting its reproduction" (*Illuminations*: 223). For Benjamin, curiosity, as an approach to the world, expands and enriches human perceptive capabilities. The mobile vision of the curious ones, made possible through the *mass-*

media, does not limit itself to taking in a given spectacle passively; on the contrary, it decides anew each time what to watch, what deserves to come to the foreground and what should remain in the background. The media trains the senses to *consider the known as if it were unknown*, to distinguish "an enormous and sudden margin of freedom" even in the most trite and repetitive aspects of daily life. At the same time, however, the media trains the senses also for the opposite task: *to consider the unknown as if it were known*, to become familiar with the unexpected and the surprising, to become accustomed to the lack of established habits.

Let us look at another significant analogy. For both Heidegger and Benjamin, those who are curious are forever *distracted*. They watch, learn, try out everything, but without paying attention. And in this regard as well, the judgment of the two authors diverges. For Heidegger, distraction, which is the correlate of curiosity, is the evident proof of a total uprooting and of a total unauthenticity. The distracted are those who pursue possibilities which are always different, but equal and interchangeable (opportunists in the prior meaning of the word, if you like). On the contrary, Benjamin clearly praises distraction itself, distinguishing in it the most effective means for taking in an artificial experience, technically constructed. He writes: "Distraction [...] presents a covert control of the extent to which new tasks have become soluble by apperception. [...] The film makes the cult value recede into the background [that is to say, the cult for a work of art which is considered to be something unique] not only by putting the public in the position of the critic [deciding what is background and what is, instead, foreground, as we discussed earlier], but also by the fact that at the movies this position requires no attention. The public [or, if you prefer: the multitude as public] is an examiner, but an absent minded one" (ibid., 240–241; comments in brackets by Virno).

It goes without saying that distraction is an obstacle to *intellectual* learning. Things change radically, however, if *sensory* learning is put into play: this type of learning is absolutely favored and empowered by distraction; it lays claim to a certain level of dispersion and inconstancy. Thus, mass media curiosity is the sensory learning of technically reproducible artifices, the immediate perception of intellectual products, the corporeal vision of scientific paradigms. The senses—or better, the "greed of sight"—succeed in appropriating an abstract reality, that is to say, concepts materialized in technology; and they do so *not* leaning forward with curiosity *but* making a showy display of distraction.

Thus, (absent-minded) curiosity and (non-referential) idle talk are attributes of the contemporary multitude: attributes loaded with ambivalence, naturally; but unavoidable attributes.

Ten Theses on the Multitude and Post-Fordist Capitalism

Day Four

I have attempted to describe the nature of contemporary production, so-called post-Fordism, on the basis of categories drawn from political philosophy, ethics, epistemology, and the philosophy of language. I have done so not as a professional exercise, but because I am truly convinced that, in order for it to be described clearly, the mode of contemporary production demands *this* variety of analyses, *this* breadth of views. One cannot understand post-Fordism without having recourse to a cluster of ethical-linguistic concepts. As is obvious, moreover, this is where the *matter of fact* lies in the progressive identification between poiesis and language, production and communication.

In order to name with a unifying term the forms of life and the linguistic games which characterize our era, I have used the notion of "multitude." This notion, the polar opposite of that of "people," is defined by a complex of breaks, landslides, and innovations which I have tried to point out. Let me cite some of them here, in no particular order: the life of the stranger (*bios xenikos*) being experienced as an ordinary condition; the prevalence of "common places" in discourse over "special" places; the publicness of the intellect, as much an apotropaic device as a pillar of social production; activity without end product (that is, virtuosity); the centrality of the principle of individuation; the relation with the possible in as much as it is possible (opportunism); the hypertrophic development of the non-referential aspects of language (idle talk). In the multitude there is a full *historical*, phenomenological, empirical display of the ontological condition of the human animal: biological artlessness, the indefinite or *potential* character of its existence, lack of a determined environment, the linguistic intellect as "compensation" for the shortage of specialized instincts. It is as if the root has risen to the surface, finally revealing itself to the naked eye. That which has always been true, is only now unveiled. The multitude is this: a fundamental biological configuration which becomes a historically determined way of being, ontology revealing itself phenomenologically. One could even say that the post-Fordist multitude manifests *anthropogenesis* as such on a historical-empirical level; that is to say, the genesis itself of the human animal, its distinguishing characteristics. The multitude epitomizes this genesis, it sums it up. Upon reflection, these rather abstract considerations are only another way of saying that the primary productive resource of contemporary capitalism lies in the linguistic-relational abilities of humankind, in the complex of communicative and cognitive faculties (*dynameis*, powers) which distinguish humans.

Our seminar is now over. That which could be said, has been (either well or poorly) said. Now, at the end of our circumnavigation of the continent of the "multitude," we need only to insist upon a few qualifying aspects of our analysis. Towards that end, I propose ten statements on the multitude and post-Fordist capitalism. I call these statements *theses* only for the sake of convenience. They do not claim to be exhaustive, nor do they seek to oppose other possible analyses or definitions of post-Fordism. They have only the apodiptic appearance, and (I hope) the precision of authentic theses. Some of these statements could possibly have converged, making of themselves one "thesis." Furthermore, the sequence is arbitrary: that which figures as "thesis x" would lose nothing if it figured as "thesis y" (and vice versa). Finally, it must be understood that often I affirm or deny with more precision, or less nuance, than what might be correct or (prudent) to do. In some cases I *shall say* more than I *think*.

Thesis 1

> *Post-Fordism (and with it the multitude) appeared, in Italy, with the social unrest which is generally remembered as the "movement of 1977."*

Post-Fordism, in Italy arose from the tumults of labor-power which was educated, uncertain, mobile; one which hated the work ethic and opposed, at times head on, the tradition and the culture of the historical left, marking a clear discontinuity with respect to assembly-line workers, with their practices and customs, with their ways of life. Post-Fordism arose from conflicts centered upon social figures which, despite their apparent marginal status, were about to become the authentic fulcrum of the new cycle of capitalistic development. Besides, it had already happened before that a radical revolution in the manner of production was accompanied by premature political strife among those strata of labor-power which, a little later, would make up the supporting axis of the production of surplus-value. It is enough to recall the dangerousness attributed in the eighteenth century to the British vagabonds, *already* thrown out of the fields and *on the verge* of being let in to the first factories. Or think of the struggles of the unskilled American workers from 1910 to 1920, struggles which preceded the Henry Ford and Frederick Taylor turning point, a turning point based precisely on the systematic removal of skill from labor. Every drastic metamorphosis of productive organization is destined from the start, to conjure up the pangs of the "original accumulation," forcing, all over again, the transformation of a relationship among *things* (new technologies, a different allocation of investments, etc.) into a *social* relationship. It is exactly in this delicate interval that, at times, the *subjective aspect*, which will later become an irrefutable course of fact, reveals itself.

The masterpiece of Italian capitalism consists of having transformed into a productive resource precisely those modes of behavior which, at first, made their appearance under the semblance of radical conflict. The conversion of the collective propensities of the 1977 movement (exit from the factories, indifference to steady employment, familiarity with learning and communication networks) into a renewed concept of professionalism (opportunism, idle talk, virtuosity, etc.): this is the most precious result of the Italian *counter-revolution* ("counter-revolution" meaning not the simple restoration of a previous state of affairs, but, literally, a *revolution to the contrary*, that is, a drastic innovation of the economy and institutions in order to re-launch productivity and political domination).

The 1977 movement had the misfortune of being treated as if it were a movement of marginal people and parasites. However, marginal and parasitical was the point of view adopted by those making these accusations. In fact, they identified themselves entirely with the Fordist paradigm, believing that only a secure job in factories making lasting consumer goods was "central" and "productive." Thus they identified with a production cycle already in decline. Looking at it closely, the 1977 movement anticipated certain traits of the post-Fordist multitude. As angry and coarse as it was, however, the virtuosity of this movement was not servile.

Thesis 2

Post-Fordism is the empirical realization of the "Fragment on Machines" by Marx.

Marx writes: "*The theft of alien labour time, on which the present wealth is based,* appears a miserable foundation in face of this new one [(the automated system of machines) Virno addition, trans.] created by large-scale industry itself. As soon as labour in the direct form has ceased to be the great well-spring of wealth, labour time ceases and must cease to be its measure, and hence exchange value [must cease to be the measure] of use value. (Italics and brackets from Nicolaus's English translation, trans.)" (*Grundrisse*: 705). In the "Fragment on Machines" from the *Grundrisse*, from which I drew that citation, Marx upholds a thesis that is hardly Marxist: abstract knowledge—scientific knowledge, first and foremost, but not only that—moves towards becoming nothing less than the principal productive force, relegating parceled and repetitive labor to a residual position. We know that Marx turns to a fairly suggestive image to indicate the complex of knowledge which makes up the epicenter of social production and at the same time prearranges its vital confines: *general intellect.* The tendential pre-eminence of knowledge makes of labor time a "miserable foundation." The so-called "law of value" (according to which the value of a product is determined by the amount of labor time that went into it), which Marx considers the keystone of modern social relations, is, however, shattered and refuted by capitalist development itself.

It is at this point that Marx proposes a hypothesis on surpassing the rate of dominant production which is very different from the more famous hypotheses presented in his other works. In the "Fragment," the crisis of capitalism is *no longer* attributed to the disproportions inherent in a means of production truly based on labor time supplied by individuals (it is no longer attributed, therefore, to the imbalances connected to the full force of the law, for example, to the fall of the rate of profit). Instead, there comes to the foreground the splitting contradiction between a productive process which directly and exclusively calls upon science, and a unit of measurement of wealth which still coincides with the quantity of labor incorporated in the products. The progressive widening of *this* differential means, according to Marx, that "production based on exchange value breaks down" (*Grundrisse*: 705) and leads thus to communism.

What is most obvious in the post-Ford era is the full factual realization of the tendency described by Marx without, however, any emancipating consequences. The disproportion between the role accomplished by knowledge and the decreasing importance of labor time has given rise to new and stable forms of power, rather than to a hotbed of crisis. The radical metamorphosis of the very concept of production belongs, as always, in the sphere of working under a boss. More than alluding to the overcoming of what already exists, the "Fragment" is a toolbox for the sociologist. It describes an empirical reality which lies in front of all our eyes: the empirical reality of the post-Fordist structure.

Thesis 3

The crisis of the society of labor is reflected in the multitude itself.

The crisis of the society of labor certainly does not coincide with a linear shrinking of labor time. Instead, the latter exhibits an unheard of pervasiveness in today's world. The positions of Gorz and Rifkin on the "end of work" (Gorz, *Reclaiming Work*; Rifkin, *The End of Work*) are mistaken; they spread misunderstandings of all kinds; and even worse, they prevent us from focusing on the very question they raise.

The crisis of the society of labor consists in the fact (brought up in thesis 2) that social wealth is produced from science, from the *general intellect*, rather than from the work delivered by individuals. The work demanded seems reducible to a virtually negligible portion of a life. Science, information, knowledge in general, cooperation, these present themselves as the key support system of production—these, rather than labor time. Nevertheless, this labor time continues to be valid as a parameter of social development and of social wealth. Thus, the overflow of labor from society establishes a contradictory process, a theater of violent oppositions and disturbing paradoxes. Labor time is the unit of measurement *in use*, but no longer the *true* one unit of measurement. To ignore one or the other of the two sides—that is, to emphasize either the validity alone, or the lack of veracity alone—does not take us far: in the first case, one does not become aware of the crisis of the society of labor, in the second case one ends up guaranteeing conciliatory representations in the manner of Gorz or Rifkin.

The surpassing of the society of labor occurs in the forms prescribed by the social system based on wage labor. Overtime, which is a potential source of wealth, manifests itself as poverty: wages compensation, structural unemployment (brought on by investments, not by the lack thereof), unlimited flexibility in the use of labor-power, proliferation of hierarchies, re-establishment of archaic disciplinary measures to control individuals no longer subject to the rules of the factory system. This is the magnetic storm which allows, on the phenomenological plane, for the "surpassing" which is paradoxical to the point of taking place upon the very foundation of that which was to be surpassed.

Let me repeat the key-phrase: the surpassing of the society of labor comes about in compliance with the rules of wage labor. This phrase can be applied to the post-Fordist situation in the same manner as Marx's observation regarding the first stock companies. Marx writes: "the joint-stock system [...] is an abolition of capitalist private industry on the basis of the capitalist system itself" (*Capital*, Volume 3: 570). That is to say: the stock companies assert the possibility of escaping the regime of private property, but this assertion always takes place within the realm of private property and, indeed, increases disproportionately the power of the latter. The difficulty, with reference to post-Fordism as well as to the stock companies, lies in considering simultaneously the two contradictory points of view, that is to say, subsistence and ending, validity and surmountability.

The crisis of the society of labor (if correctly understood) implies that *all of* post-Fordist labor-power can be described using the categories with which Marx analyzed the "industrial reserve army," that is, unemployment. Marx believed that the "industrial reserve army" was divisible into three types or figures: *fluid* (today we would speak of turn-over, early retirement, etc.), *latent* (where at any moment a technological innovation could intervene, reducing employment), *stagnant* (in current terms: working under the table, temporary work, atypical work). According to Marx, it is the mass of the unemployed which is fluid, latent or stagnant, certainly not the *employed* labor class; they are a marginal sector of labor-power, not its main sector. Yet, the crisis of the society of labor (with the complex characteristics which I tried to outline earlier) causes these three determining categories to apply, in effect, to all labor-power. Fluid, or latent, or stagnant, applies to the employed labor class as such. Each allocation of wage labor allows the non-necessity of that labor and the excessive social cost inherent in that labor to leak out. But this non-necessity, as always, manifests itself as a perpetuation of wage labor in temporary or "flexible" forms.

Thesis 4

For the post-Fordist multitude every qualitative difference between labor time and non-labor time falls short.

Social time, in today's world, seems to have come unhinged because there is no longer anything which distinguishes labor from the rest of human activities. Therefore, since work ceases to constitute a special and separate praxis, with distinctive criteria and procedures in effect at its center, completely different from those criteria and procedures which regulate non-labor time, there is not a clean, well-defined threshold separating labor time from non-labor time. In Fordism, according to Gramsci, the intellect remains outside of production; only when the work has been finished does the Fordist worker read the newspaper, go to the local party headquarters, think, have conversations. In post-Fordism, however, since the "life of the mind" is included fully within the time-space of production, an essential homogeneity prevails.

Labor and non-labor develop an identical form of productivity, based on the exercise of generic human faculties: language, memory, sociability, ethical and aesthetic inclinations, the capacity for abstraction and learning. From the point of view of "what" is done and "how" it is done, there is no substantial difference between employment and unemployment. It could be said that: unemployment is non-remunerated labor and labor, in turn, is remunerated unemployment. Working endlessly can be justified with good reasons, and working less and less frequently can be equally justified. These paradoxical formulas, contradicting each other, when put together demonstrate how social time has come unhinged.

The old distinction between "labor" and "non-labor" ends up in the distinction between remunerated life and non-remunerated life. The border between these two lives is arbitrary, changeable, subject to political decision making.

The productive cooperation in which labor-power participates is always larger and richer than the one put into play by the labor process. It includes also the world of non-labor, the experiences and knowledge matured outside of the factory and the office. Labor-power increases the value of capital only because it never loses its qualities of non-labor (that is, its inherent connection to a productive cooperation richer than the one implicit in the labor process in the strictest sense of the term).

Since social cooperation precedes and exceeds the work process, post-Fordist labor is always, also, *hidden labor*. This expression should not be taken here to mean labor which is un-contracted, "under the table." Hidden labor is, in the first place, non-remunerated life, that is to say the part of human activity which, alike in every respect to the activity of labor, is not, however, calculated as productive force.

The crucial point here is to recognize that in the realm of labor, experiences which mature outside of labor hold predominant weight; at the same time, we must be aware that this more general sphere of experience, once included in the productive process, is subordinate to the rules of the mode of capitalistic production. Here also there is a double risk: either to deny the breadth of what is included in the mode of production, or, in the name of this breadth, to deny the existence of a specific mode of production.

Thesis 5

In post-Fordism there exists a permanent disproportion between "labor time" and the more ample "production time."

Marx distinguishes between "labor time" and "production time" in chapters XII and XIII of the second book of the *Capital.* Think of the cycle of sowing and harvesting. The farm laborer works for a month (labor time); then a long interval follows for the growing of the grain (production time, but no longer labor time); and at last, the period of harvesting arrives (once again, labor time). In agriculture and other sectors, production is more extensive than labor activity, in the proper sense of the term; the latter makes up hardly a fraction of the overall cycle. The pairing of the terms "labor time"/ "production time" is an extraordinarily pertinent conceptual tool for understanding post-Fordist reality, that is to say, the modern expression of the social working day. Beyond the examples from agriculture adopted by Marx, the disproportion between "production" and "labor" fits fairly well the situation described in "Fragment on Machines"; in other words, it fits a situation in which labor time presents itself as "miserable residue."

The disproportion takes on two different forms. In the first place, it is revealed within every single working day of every single worker. The worker oversees and coordinates (labor time) the automatic system of machines (whose function defines production time); the worker's activity often ends up being a sort of *maintenance.* It could be said that in the post-Fordist environment production time is interrupted only at intervals by labor time. While sowing is a necessary condition for the subsequent phase of the grain's growth, the modern activity of overseeing and coordinating is placed, from beginning to end, *alongside* the automated process.

There is a second, and more radical, way of conceiving this disproportion. In post-Fordism "production time" includes non-labor time, during which social cooperation takes its root (see thesis 4). Hence I define "production time" as that indissoluble unity of remunerated life and non-remunerated life, labor and non-labor, emerged social cooperation and submerged social cooperation. "Labor time" is only one component, and not necessarily the most prominent one, of "production time" understood in this way. This evidence drives us to reformulate, in part or entirely, the theory of surplus-value. According to Marx, surplus-value springs from surplus-labor, that is, from the difference between necessary labor (which compensates the capitalist for the expense sustained in acquiring the labor-power) and the entirety of the working day. So then, one would have to say that in the post-Fordist era, surplus-value is determined above all by the gap between production time which is not calculated as labor time and labor time in the true sense of the term. What matters is not only the disproportion, inherent in labor time, between necessary labor and surplus-labor, but also, and perhaps even more, the disproportion between production time (which includes non-labor, its own distinctive productivity) and labor time.

Thesis 6

In one way, post-Fordism is characterized by the co-existence of the most diverse productive models and, in another way, by essentially homogeneous socialization which takes place outside of the workplace.

Differently from the Fordist organization of labor, today's organization of labor is always spotty. Technological innovation is not universal: more than determining an unequivocal and leading productive model, it keeps a myriad of different models alive, including the resuscitation of some outdated and anachronistic models. Post-Fordism re-edits the entire history of labor, from islands of mass labor to *enclaves* of professional workers, from re-inflated independent labor to reinstated forms of personal power. The production models which have followed one another during this long period re-present themselves *synchronically*, as if according to the standards of a World's Fair. The background and the hypothesis behind this proliferation of differences, this shattering of organizing forms, is established, however, by the general intellect, by computerized data communication technology, by productive cooperation which includes within itself the time of non-labor. Paradoxically, just when knowledge and language become the principal productive force, there is an unrestrained multiplication of the models of labor organization, not to mention their eclectic co-existence.

We may well ask what the software engineer has in common with the Fiat worker, or with the temporary worker. We must have the courage to answer: precious little, with regard to job description, to professional skills, to the nature of the labor process. But we can also answer: everything, with regard to the make-up and contents of the socialization of single individuals outside of the work place. That is to say, these workers have in common emotional tonalities, interests, mentality, expectations. Except that, while in the advanced sectors this homogeneous *ethos* (opportunism, idle talk, etc.) is included in production and delineates professional profiles, this ethos strengthens, instead, the "world of life" for those who fall into the traditional sectors, as well as for the *border-workers* who swing between work and unemployment. To put it succinctly: the seam is to be found between the *opportunism at work* and the universal opportunism demanded by the urban experience. The essentially unitary character of socialization detached from the labor process stands in counterpoint to the fragmentation of productive models, to their World's Fair style co-existence.

Thesis 7

In Post-Fordism, the general intellect *does not coincide with fixed capital, but manifests itself principally as a linguistic reiteration of living labor.*

As was already said on the second day of our seminar, Marx, without reserve, equated the *general intellect* (that is, knowledge as principal productive force) with fixed capital, with the "objective scientific capacity" inherent in the system of machines. In this way he omitted the dimension, absolutely preeminent today, in which the *general intellect* presents itself as living labor. It is necessary to analyze post-Fordist production in order to support this criticism. In so-called "second-generation independent labor," but also in the operational procedures of a radically reformed factory such as the Fiat factory in Melfi, it is not difficult to recognize that the connection between knowledge and production is not at all exhausted within the system of machines; on the contrary, it articulates itself in the linguistic cooperation of men and women, in their actually acting in concert. In the Post-Fordist environment, a decisive role is played by the infinite variety of concepts and logical schemes which cannot ever be set within fixed capital, being inseparable from the reiteration of a plurality of living subjects. The *general intellect* includes, thus, formal and informal knowledge, imagination, ethical propensities, mindsets, and "linguistic games." In contemporary labor processes, there are thoughts and discourses which function as productive "machines," without having to adopt the form of a mechanical body or of an electronic valve.

The *general intellect* becomes an attribute of living labor when the activity of the latter consists increasingly of linguistic services. Here we touch upon the lack of foundation in Jürgen Habermas's position. Inspired by Hegel's teachings in Jena (Habermas, *Arbeit und Interaktion*), he contrasts labor with interaction, "instrumental or 'strategic' action" with "communicative action." In his judgment, the two spheres answer to standards that are mutually incommensurable: labor comes straight from the logic of means/ends, linguistic interaction rests upon exchange, upon reciprocal recognition, upon the sharing of an identical *ethos*. Today, however, wage labor (employed, surplus-value producing labor) *is* interaction. The labor process is no longer taciturn, but loquacious. "Communicative action" no longer holds its privileged, even exclusive, place within ethical-cultural relations or within politics, no longer lies outside the sphere of the material reproduction of life. To the contrary, the dialogical word is seated at the very heart of capitalistic production. In short: to understand fully the rules of post-Fordist labor, it is necessary to turn more and more to Saussure and Wittgenstein. It is true that these authors lost interest in the social relations of production; nevertheless, since they reflected so deeply on linguistic experience, they have more to teach us about the "loquacious factory" than do the professional economists.

It has already been stated that one part of the labor time of an individual is destined to enrich and strengthen productive cooperation itself, the mosaic in which the individual serves as one tessera. To put it more clearly: the task of a worker is that of rendering better and more varied the connection between individual labor and the services of others. It is this *reflective* character of labor activity which insists that in labor the linguistic-relational aspects assume an increasing importance; it also insists that opportunism and idle talk become tools of great importance. Hegel spoke of an "astuteness of labor," meaning by this expression the capacity to further natural causality, with the aim of utilizing its power in view of a determined goal. Accordingly, in the realm of post-Fordism, Hegel's "astuteness" has been supplanted by Heidegger's "idle talk."

Thesis 8

> *The whole of post-Fordist labor-power, even the most unskilled, is an intellectual labor-power, the "intellectuality of the masses."*

I use the term "intellectuality of the masses" for the whole of post-Ford era living labor (not including certain specially qualified industries of the tertiary sector) in that it is a depository of cognitive and communicative skills which cannot be objectified within the system of machines. The intellectuality of the masses is the preeminent form in which, today, the *general intellect* reveals itself (see thesis 7). I hardly need to say that I do not refer in any way to any imaginary erudition of subordinate labor; I certainly do not think that today's workers are experts in the fields of molecular biology or classical philology. As was already mentioned in the preceding days, what stands out is rather the *intellect in general*, the most generic aptitudes of the mind: the faculty of language, the inclination to learn, memory, the ability to abstract and to correlate, the inclination toward self-reflection. The intellectuality of the masses has nothing to do with *acts* of thought (books, algebraic formulas, etc.) but with the simple *faculty* of thought and verbal communication. Language (like intellect or memory) is much more diffuse and less specialized than what has been thought. It is not the scientists, but the simple speakers who are a good example of the intellectuality of the masses. They have nothing to do with the new "worker aristocracy"; rather, they stand at the opposite pole. Upon close reflection, the intellectuality of the masses does nothing less than prove completely true, for the first time, the Marxist definition of labor-power already cited: "the aggregate of those mental and physical capabilities existing in the physical form, the living personality, of a human being" (*Capital*, Volume 1: 270).

With regard to the intellectuality of the masses, it is necessary to avoid those deadly simplifications that befall those who are always searching for comfortable repetitions of past experiences. A way of being that has its fulcrum in knowledge and language cannot be defined according to economic-productive categories. In sum, we are not dealing here with the last link of that chain whose preceding links are, as far as I know, the worker by trade and the assembly-line worker. The characteristic aspects of the intellectuality of the masses, its identity, so to speak, cannot be found in relation to labor, but, above all, on the level of life forms, of cultural consumption, of linguistic practices. Nevertheless, and this is the other side of the coin, just when production is no longer in any way the specific locus of the formation of identity, *exactly at that point* does it project itself into every aspect of experience, subsuming linguistic competencies, ethical propensities, and the nuances of subjectivity.

The intellectuality of the masses lies at the heart of this dialectic. Because it is difficult to describe in economic-productive terms, for this reason exactly (and not in spite of this reason), it is a fundamental component of today's capitalistic accumulation. The intellectuality of the masses (another name for the multitude) is at the center of the post-Ford economy precisely because its mode of being completely avoids the concepts of the political economy.

Thesis 9

The multitude throws the "theory of proletarianization" out of the mix.

In Marxist theoretical discussion, the comparison between "complex" (intellectual, that is) labor and "simple" (unskilled) labor has provoked more than a few problems. What is the unit of measurement which permits this comparison? The prevalent answer is: the unit of measurement coincides with "simple" labor, along with the pure waste of psychophysical energy; "complex" labor is merely a multiple of "simple" labor. The ratio between one and the other can be determined by considering the different cost of education (school, varied specializations, etc.) for the intellectual labor-power as opposed to the unskilled labor-power. Little of this old and controversial question interests me; here I would like, however, to capitalize on the terminology used in its regard. I hold that the intellectuality of the masses (see thesis 8) in its totality is "complex" labor—but, note carefully—"complex" labor which is *not reducible* to "simple" labor. The complexity, as well as the irreducibility, comes from the fact that this labor-power mobilizes, in the fulfilling of its work duties, linguistic-cognitive competencies which are generically human. These competencies, or faculties, cause the duties of the individual to be characterized *always* by a high rate of sociability and intelligence, even though they are not all specialized duties (we are not speaking of engineers or philologists here, but of ordinary workers). That which is not reducible to "simple" labor is, if you will, the *cooperative quality* of the concrete operations carried out by the intellectuality of the masses.

To say that all post-Ford era labor is complex labor, irreducible to simple labor, means also to confirm that today the "theory of proletarianization" is completely out of the mix. This theory had its peak of honor in signaling the potential comparability of intellectual labor to manual labor. Precisely for this reason, the theory ends up unsuited for accounting for the intellectuality of the masses or, and this is the same thing, for accounting for living labor as *general intellect*. The theory of proletarianization fails when intellectual (or complex) labor cannot be equated with a network of specialized knowledge, but becomes one with the use of the generic linguistic-cognitive faculties of the human animal. This is the conceptual (and practical) movement which modifies all the terms of the question.

The lack of proletarianization certainly does not mean that qualified workers retain privileged niches. Instead it means that the sort of *homogeneity by subtraction* which the concept of "proletariat" usually implies does not characterize all post-Fordist labor-power, as complex or intellectual as it may be. In other words, the lack of proletarianization means that post-Ford labor is *multitude*, not *people*.

Thesis 10

Post-Fordism is the "communism of capital."

The metamorphosis of social systems in the West, during the 1930's, has at times been designated with an expression as clear as it is apparently paradoxical: *socialism of capital.* With this term one alludes to the determining role taken on by the State within the economic cycle, to the end of the *laissez-faire* liberalist, to the processes of centralization and planning guided by public industry, to the politics of full employment, to the beginning of *Welfare.* The capitalistic response to the October Revolution and the crisis of 1929 was the gigantic socialization (or better, nationalization) of the means of production. To put it in the words of Marx which I cited a little while ago, there was "an abolition of the capitalist private industry on the basis of the capitalist system itself" (*Capital*, Volume 3: 570).

The metamorphosis of social systems in the West, during the 1980's and 1990's, can be synthesized in a more pertinent manner with the expression: *communism of capital.* This means that the capitalistic initiative orchestrates for its own benefit precisely those material and cultural conditions which would guarantee a calm version of realism for the potential communist. Think of the objectives which constitute the fulcrum of such a prospect: the abolition of that intolerable scandal, the persistence of wage labor; the extinction of the State as an industry of coercion and as a "monopoly of political decision-making"; the valorization of all that which renders the life of an individual unique. Yet, in the course of the last twenty years, an insidious and terrible interpretation of these same objectives has been put forth. First of all, the irreversible shrinking of socially necessary labor time has taken place, with an increase in labor time for those on the "inside" and the alienation of those on the "outside." Even when squeezed by temporary workers, the entity of employed workers presents itself as "overpopulation" or as the "industrial reserve army." Secondly, the radical crisis, or actually the desegregation, of the national States expresses itself as the miniature reproduction, like a Chinese box, of the form-of-State. Thirdly, after the fall of a "universal equivalent" capable of operating effectively, we witness a fetishistic cult of *differences*—except that these differences, claiming a substantial surreptitious foundation, give rise to all sorts of domineering and discriminating hierarchies.

If we can say that Fordism incorporated, and rewrote in its own way, some aspects of the socialist experience, then post-Fordism has fundamentally dismissed both Keynesianism *and* socialism. Post-Fordism, hinging as it does upon the *general intellect* and the multitude, puts forth, *in its own way*, typical demands of communism (abolition of work, dissolution of the State, etc.). Post-Fordism is the communism of capital.

Following on the heels of the Ford era, there was the socialist revolution in Russia (and, even if defeated, an attempt at revolution in western Europe). It is appropriate to ask which experience of social unrest served as the prelude to post-Fordism. Well, I believe that during the 1960's and 1970's there was, in the West, a defeated revolution—the first revolution aimed not against poverty and backwardness, but specifically against the means of capitalistic production, thus, against wage labor. If I speak of a defeated revolution, it is not because a lot of people were blathering on about revolution. I am not referring to the circus of subjectivity, but to a sober fact: for a long period of time, both in the factories and in the lower income urban areas, in the schools as in certain fragile state institutions, two opposing powers confronted one another, resulting in the paralysis of political decision-making. From this point of view—objective, serious—it can be maintained that in Italy and in other Western countries there was a defeated revolution. Post-Fordism, or the "communism of capital," is the answer to *this* defeated revolution, so different from those of the 1920's. The quality of the "answer" is equal to and opposed to the quality of the "question." I believe that the social struggles of the 1960's and 1970's expressed non-socialist demands, indeed anti-socialist demands: radical criticism of labor; an accentuated taste for differences, or, if you prefer, a refining of the "principle of individuation"; no longer the desire to take possession of the State, but the aptitude (at times violent, certainly) for defending oneself from the State, for dissolving the bondage to the State as such. It is not difficult to recognize communist inspiration and orientation in the failed revolution of the 1960's and 1970's. For this reason, post-Fordism, which constitutes a response to that revolution, has given life to a sort of paradoxical "communism of capital."

BIBLIOGRAPHY

Only those works mentioned in the course of the seminar are listed below. The bibliographical information found in the text refers to the English translations unless otherwise indicated.

Adorno, Theodor W., and Max Horckheimer. *Dialektik der Aufklärung* (1947). *Dialectic of Enlightenment*, translated by John Cumming, New York: Herder and Herder, 1972.

Arendt, Hannah. *The Human Condition*. Chicago: The University of Chicago Press, 1958.

Arendt, Hannah. *Between Past and Future: Eight Exercises in Political Thought*. New York: Viking Press, 1968.

Aristotle. *Nicomachean Ethics* in *The Basic Works of Aristotle*, edited by Richard McKeon, NewYork: Random House, 1941.

Aristotle. *Rhetoric* in *The Basic Works of Aristotle*, edited by Richard McKeon, New York: Random House, 1941.

Aristotle. *Protrepticus: A Reconstruction*, edited by Anton-Hermann Chroust, Notre Dame, Indiana: University of Notre Dame Press, 1964.

Augustinus, Aurelius [Augustine of Hippo]. *Confessiones* (401 c.e.). *Confessions*, translated by R.S. Pine-Coffin, London: Penguin Books, 1961.

Austin, John L. *How to Do Things with Words*. Cambridge: Harvard University Press, 1962.

Bachelard, Gaston. *La philosophie du non: Essai d'une philosophie du nouvel esprit scientifique* (1940). *The Philosophy of No: A Philosophy of the New Scientific Mind*, translated by G. C. Waterston, New York: The Orion Press, 1968.

Benjamin, Walter. "Das Kunstwerk im Zeitalter seiner technischen Reproduzierbarkeit" in *Illuminationen* (1936). "The Work of Art in the Age of Mechanical Reproduction" in *Illuminations*, translated by Harry Zohn, edited by Hannah Arendt, New York: Schocken Books, 1969.

Benveniste, Emile. "L'appareil formel de l'énonciation" in *Problèmes de linguistique générale* (1970). *Problems in General Linguistics,* translated by Mary Elizabeth Meek, Coral Gables,

Florida: University of Miami Press: 1997.

Bianciardi, Luciano. *La vita agra*. Milano: Rizzoli, 1962.

Debord, Guy. *La société du spectacle* (1967). *Society of the Spectacle*, translated by Donald Nicholson-Smith, New York: Zone Books, 1994.

Foucault, Michel. *Résumé des cours 1970–1982*. Paris: Julliard, 1989.

Freud, Sigmund. "Das Unheimliche" (1919). "The Uncanny," translation by Alix Strachey in *Sigmund Freud, Collected Papers, Vol.4*. New York: Basic Books, 1959.

Gehlen, Arnold. *Der Mensch. Seine Natur und seine Stellung in der Welt* (1940). *Man: His Nature and Place in the World*, translated by Clare McMillan and Karl Pillemer, New York: Columbia University Press, 1988.

Gould, Glenn. *The Glenn Gould Reader*, edited by Tim Page, New York: Knopf, 1984.

Gorz, André. *Misères du présent, richesse du possible* (1997). *Reclaiming Work: Beyond the Wage-based Society*, translated by Chris Turner, Cambridge, England: Polity Press, 1999.

Habermas, Jürgen. "Arbeit und Interaktion" in *Technik und Wissenschaft als 'Ideologie'*. Frankfurt am Main: Suhrkamp, 1968.

Heidegger, Martin. *Sein und Zeit* (1927). *Being and Time*, translated by John Macquarrie and Edward Robinson, New York: Harper and Row, 1962.

Hirschman, Albert O. *Exit, Voice and Loyalty*. Cambridge, Massachusetts: Harvard University Press, 1970.

Hobbes, Thomas. *De Cive* (1642), edited by Sterling P. Lamprecht, New York: Appleton-Century-Crofts, 1949.

Hobbes, Thomas. *Leviathan* (1651), edited by Michael Oakeshott, Oxford: Basil Blackwell, 1957.

Kant, Immanuel. *Kritik der Urtheilskraft* (1790). *Critique of Judgment*, translated by Werner S. Pluhar, Indianapolis, Indiana: Hackett Publishers, 1987.

Marx, Karl. *Oekonomisch-philosophische Manuskripte aus dem Jahre* 1844 (1932). *The Economic and Philosophic Manuscripts of 1844*, translated by Martin Milligan, edited by Dirk J. Struik, New York: International Publishers, 1964.

Marx, Karl. *Grundrisse der politischen Oekonomie* (1939-1941). *Grundrisse*, translated by Martin Nicolaus, London: Penguin Books, 1973.

Marx, Karl. *Das Kapital* (1867). *Capital*, Volume 1, translated by Ben Fowkes, London: Penguin Books, 1990; Volume 2, translated by David Fernbach, London: Penguin Books, 1992; Volume 3, translated by David Fernbach, London: Penguin Books, 1991.

Marx, Karl. *Theorien über den Mehrwert* (1905). *Theories of Surplus-value*, translated by Emile Burns, edited by S. Ryazanskaya, Moscow: Progress Publishers, 1969.

Merleau-Ponty, Maurice. *Phénoménologie de la perception* (1945). *Phenomenology of Perception*, translated by Colin Smith, New York: Humanities Press, 1962.

Rifkin, Jeremy. *The End of Work*. New York: G. P. Putnam's Sons, 1996.

Saussure, Ferdinand de. *Cours de linguistique générale* (1922). *Course in General Linguistics*, translated by Roy Harris, edited by Charles Bally and Albert Riedlinger, LaSalle, Illinois: Open Court, 1986.

Schmitt, Carl. *Der Begriff des Politischen: Text von 1932 mit einem Vorwort und drei Corollarien* (1963). *The Concept of the Political*, translated by George Schwab, Chicago: The University of Chicago Press, 1996.

Schneider, Michel. *Glenn Gould. Piano solo. Aria et trente variations*. Paris: Gallimard, 1988.

Simondon, Gilbert. *L'individuation psychique et collective*. Paris: Aubier, 1989.

Spinoza, Benedictus (Baruch). *Tractatus Politicus* (1677), translated by Samuel Shirley, Indianapolis, Indiana: Hackett Publishers, 2000.

Virno, Paolo. *Mondanità. L'idea di mondo tra esperienza sensibile e sfera pubblica*. Roma: Manifestolibri, 1994.

Virno, Paolo. *Il ricordo del presente. Saggio sul tempo storico*. Torino: Bollati Boringhieri, 1999.

Weber, Max. *Politik als Beruf* (1919). *Politics as a Vocation*, translated by H. H. Gerth and C. Wright Mills, Philadelphia: Fortress Press, 1965.

Index

SEMIOTEXT(E) • NATIVE AGENTS SERIES
Chris Kraus, *Editor*

Airless Spaces Shulamith Firestone
Aliens & Anorexia Chris Kraus
Hannibal Lecter, My Father Kathy Acker
How I Became One of the Invisible David Rattray
If You're a Girl Anne Rower
I Love Dick Chris Kraus
Indivisible Fanny Howe
Leash Jane DeLynn
The Madame Realism Complex Lynne Tillman
The New Fuck You: Adventures In Lesbian Reading Eileen Myles & Liz Kotz, eds
Not Me Eileen Myles
The Origin of the Species Barbara Barg
The Pain Journal Bob Flanagan
The Passionate Mistakes and Intricate Corruption of One Girl in America Michelle Tea
Reading Brooke Shields: The Garden of Failure Eldon Garnet
Walking Through Clear Water in a Pool Painted Black Cookie Mueller

SEMIOTEXT(E) • DOUBLE AGENTS SERIES
Sylvère Lotringer, *Editor*

Aesthetics of Disappearance Paul Virilio
Archeology of Violence Pierre Clastres
Burroughs Live (The Collected Interviews) Sylvère Lotringer, ed.
Desert Islands and Other Texts (1953-1974) Gilles Deleuze
Fatal Strategies Jean Baudrillard
Foucault Live: Collected Interviews of Michel Foucault Sylvère Lotringer, ed.
Hatred of Capitalism: a Semiotext(e) Reader Chris Kraus & Sylvère Lotringer, eds.
Lost Dimension Paul Virilio

SEMIOTEXT(E) • THE JOURNAL
Sylvère Lotringer, *Editor*

Imported: A Reading Seminar Rainer Ganahl, ed.
Polysexuality Francois Péraldi, ed.
Autonomia: Post-Politics Politics Sylvère Lotringer & Christian Marazzi, Eds
Schizo-culture Sylvère Lotringer, ed.

SEMIOTEXT(E) • FOREIGN AGENTS SERIES

Sylvère Lotringer, *Editor*

The Accident of Art Sylvère Lotringer & Paul Virilio
Chaosophy Félix Guattari
Crepuscular Dawn Paul Virilio & Sylvère Lotringer
Driftworks Jean-François Lyotard
Ecstasy of Communication Jean Baudrillard
Fearless Speech Michel Foucault
Forget Foucault Jean Baudrillard
Germania Heiner Müller
A Grammar of the Multitude Paolo Virno
Inside & Out of Byzantium Nina Zivancevic
In the Shadow of the Silent Majorities Jean Baudrillard
Looking Back on the End of the World Jean Baudrillard, Paul Virilio, et al.
Nomadology: The War Machine Gilles Deleuze & Félix Guattari
On The Line Gilles Deleuze & Félix Guattari
Politics of the Very Worst Paul Virilio
The Politics of Truth Michel Foucault
Popular Defense and Ecological Struggles Paul Virilio
Pure War Paul Virilio & Sylvère Lotringer
Revolt, She Said Julia Kristeva
Sadness at Leaving Erje Ayden
Simulations Jean Baudrillard
69 Ways to Play the Blues Jurg Laederach
Soft Subversions Félix Guattari
Speed and Politics Paul Virilio
Why Different: Luce Irigaray

SEMIOTEXT(E) • ACTIVE AGENTS SERIES

Hedi El Kholti, Chris Kraus & Sylvère Lotringer, *Editors*

The Empire of Disorder Alain Joxe
Reporting from Ramallah: An Israeli Journalist in an Occupied Land Amira Hass
Still Black, Still Strong Dhoruba Bin Wahad, Mumia Abu-Jamal & Assata Shakur

Semiotext(e) is re-issuing its legendary magazine issue, *Italy: Autonomia. Post-Political Politics.* (320 pages, Illustr.) Originally published in New York in 1980.

Edited by Sylvère Lotringer and Christian Marazzi with the direct participation of the main leaders and theorists of the autonomist movement (Toni Negri, Mario Tronti, Franco Piperno, Oreste Scalzone, Paolo Virno, Sergio Bologna, Bifo, etc.) it is the only first-hand document and live analysis that exists of the most innovative post-68 radical movement in the West. The embattled issue was meant to raise interest in the fate of the Italian autonomist's mass movement caught at the time between the forces of the governement and the "armed combattants of the proletariat" (the Red Brigades). Even after the physical elimination of Autonomia, it remains a crucial testimony of the way this creative, futuristic, neo-anarchistic, post-ideological, non-representative political mass of young workers and intellectuals movement anticipated and formulated issues that are now confronting us in the wake of Empire.